Grammar Rules!

High-Interest Activities for Practice
and Mastery of Basic
Grammar Skills

Grades 3-4

by Jillayne Prince Wallaker

Dedication

With lots of love to Maegen, Madalen, Ian, and always to Willie.

Credits

Editors:
Tracy Soles, Donna Walkush

Layout Design:
Victory Productions, Inc.

Illustrations:
Janet Armbrust

Cover Design:
Peggy Jackson

This book has been correlated to state, national, and Canadian provincial standards. Visit *www.carsondellosa.com* to search for and view its correlations to your standards.

Printed in the USA • All rights reserved.

ISBN 0-88724-976-0

03-091131151

Contents

► Contents

▶ Introduction

Some might be surprised by the title *Grammar Rules!* However, this grammar book was developed so that writing teachers can show students that grammar can be understood (and sometimes even fun) when presented in a clear, reasonable way. *Grammar Rules!* builds on each topic in a logical progression so that students learn the facts behind the skill, practice the skill, then are able to put their new grammar knowledge into action.

After each grammar skill is introduced, plenty of practice is provided, along with a Review Work and a Draft Book exercise for students to transfer their new skill. Review Work assignments focus on previously covered skills or provides additional practice with a skill on the given page. The Draft Book assignments encourage students to apply the grammar skills beyond the reproducible pages and incorporate them into their own writing. For the Draft Book activities, students can complete assignments on loose-leaf paper in a folder or in a spiral or composition notebook.

Each grammar skill presented in the Review Work and Draft Book exercises has a locator code, such as underlining nouns with yellow. This code is consistent throughout the book. This provides a student with a patterned tool for self-monitoring as well as self-editing.

This book also contains a comprehensive review on pages 112-113. These pages are perfect for a pre-lesson and post-lesson assessment or an end-of-year test.

A student editing checklist is included on pages 114-115. This page is designed to be used as a self-editing tool. By assigning two or three items to check at a time, students are not overwhelmed with "getting everything right," but instead can focus on very specific skills until they understand them completely. Once mastery of the selected editing skills is evident, an additional set of items can be assigned. The same piece of student writing can be used for several editing assignments or students can use different writing samples. This convenient checklist can be kept with each student Draft Book as a reminder of grammatical variations that can be included in their writing. It can also be used to monitor student progress by dating each skill when it is demonstrated consistently.

Grammar Rules! will quickly become a resource that writing teachers return to for strong grammar activities to show their students that grammar really does rule!

Name _____

▶ Categories

Nouns are words that name people, places, things, or ideas.

Write each noun in the correct category.

ocean	classmate	Megan	Neptune
carnival	computer	boredom	restaurant
llama	imagination	mineral	happiness
pilot	parents	peace	North America

People

_____

_____

_____

_____

_____

_____

Places

_____

_____

_____

_____

_____

_____

Things

_____

_____

_____

_____

_____

Ideas

_____

_____

_____

_____

_____

🔍 **Review Work**

Write two nouns of your own in each category.

✏️ **Draft Book**

Choose one noun from each category. Write one sentence with each noun. Underline each noun with yellow.

▶ Find the Nouns

nouns

Nouns are words that name people, places, things, or ideas.

Underline the nouns in the sentences.

Ellie has a wonderful idea.

Tarantulas live in Arizona.

Max went to the course to play golf with his brother.

That turtle in the sink belongs to Anna.

The computer printed six pages of text.

Simon always encouraged Gwen's creativity.

Ian fertilized the plants by the window.

The boots in the hallway belong to Pam.

🔍 Review Work

Write the nouns from the sentences in the correct categories.

People: _____

_____

Places: _____

_____

Things: _____

_____

Ideas: _____

_____

Draft Book

Make lists of people you know, places you have been, and things that interest you. These are all nouns! Include at least 10 nouns in each list. Use these nouns in future writing assignments.

Name _____

Common nouns are nouns that name unspecific or general people, places, things, or ideas. Proper nouns are nouns that name specific people, places, things, or ideas. A proper noun always starts with an uppercase letter. A person's first and last names are proper nouns. Titles like Mr., Mrs., Miss, Ms., and Dr. are proper nouns, too.

examples: girl, president, leader (common nouns)

examples: Sarah Berg, President Lincoln, Martin Luther King, Jr. (proper nouns)

Write each noun in the correct category. Capitalize the proper nouns.

cory	doctor	mr. prince	parent
teammate	carol hobin	dr. desmond	florida
lynette	artist	student	cook
judge	golden gate bridge	sam smith	editor

Common Nouns   **Proper Nouns**

_____   _____

_____   _____

_____   _____

_____   _____

_____   _____

_____   _____

_____   _____

_____   _____

 **Review Work**

Write two nouns of your own in each category.

 Draft Book

Write five sentences. Use a proper noun that names a person in each sentence.

▶ Pick and Fix

▶ proper nouns

Proper nouns name specific people, places, things, or ideas. A proper noun always starts with an uppercase letter.

Circle the proper noun in each set of words. Rewrite it correctly.

a house / the white house   _____

sears tower / a building   _____

mr. tabby / cat   _____

president washington / a president   _____

mrs. larchmont / a woman   _____

river / ohio river   _____

holiday / flag day   _____

maine / state   _____

city / st. petersburg   _____

beaver island / island   _____

my street / oak drive   _____

best friend / jean fry   _____

statue / statue of liberty   _____

🔍 Review Work

Write three common nouns on the top lines. Make them proper nouns on the lines below.

_____ _____ _____

_____ _____ _____

✏️ Draft Book

Make a list of at least 10 proper nouns. You can include product names. Use these nouns in future writing assignments.

Name _____

Proper nouns name specific people, places, things, or ideas. A proper noun always starts with an uppercase letter.

Which nouns in the sentences are proper nouns? For each word that needs a beginning uppercase letter, cross out the lowercase letter and write the uppercase letter above it.

The president of the company, ms. smarts, is in her office.

gutzon borglum grew up in fremont, nebraska. He designed mount rushmore.

mr. wills works for a company called build-it houses.

The white house is in washington, dc.

mount everest is located in the himalayan mountains.

dez went to bergerone, canada, to go whale watching.

jordan, haley, and maggie will ride their bikes to ottawa beach.

jenny and paul are in a play called fireflies.

That picture shows a glacier separating in glacier gorge, alaska.

Review Work

Underline the common nouns in the sentences with yellow.

Draft Book

Write five sentences using common and proper nouns. Underline all of the nouns with yellow. Capitalize the proper nouns.

Here and There ▸ proper nouns

Proper nouns name specific people, places, things, or ideas. A proper noun always starts with an uppercase letter. When proper nouns name a city and state, a comma goes between them.

example: Orlando, Florida

Write the names and addresses correctly. Capitalize the proper nouns. Put commas between the city and state names.

mr. m. t. headler   _____

9210 polk boulevard   _____

littletown ohio 45678   _____

mrs. s. o. socking   _____

86 dampness drive   _____

verywet washington 98110   _____

For each proper noun that needs a beginning uppercase letter, cross out the lowercase letter and write the uppercase letter above it. Put commas between the city and state names.

olga and ron's family plans to take a trip to portland oregon.

andrew's grandmother lives in sheboygan wisconsin.

walter stopped in pierre south dakota, on his way to mount rushmore.

 Review Work

> In the sentences, draw an X next to each proper noun that names a person. Draw a triangle above each proper noun that names a place.

 Draft Book

> Write your name and address. Capitalize all of the proper nouns. Put a comma between the names of your city and state.

Name _____

▶ Shorten It

Proper nouns name specific people, places, things, or ideas. Some proper nouns can be abbreviated, or shortened. The complete words and their abbreviations always start with uppercase letters.

example: Kyle P. Willis or K. P. W.
example: Mister Holden or Mr. Holden

Draw lines to match the nouns to their abbreviations.

company	Ave.
boulevard	Co.
street	Blvd.
avenue	USA
road	Dr.
United States of America	St.
doctor	Rd.

 Review Work

Write your full name and a friend's full name. Write the initials after the names.

_____

_____

 Draft Book

Make a list of abbreviations. Add periods to the abbreviations where they are needed. Write the complete words beside the abbreviations.

Name _____

Special Times

Days and months are proper nouns. Some of these nouns can be abbreviated. The complete words and their abbreviations always start with uppercase letters.

Draw lines to match the nouns to their abbreviations.

Saturday	Tues.	Sunday	Apr.
February	Dec.	March	Nov.
Tuesday	Aug.	April	Wed.
August	Feb.	Wednesday	Sun.
Thursday	Thurs.	September	Oct.
Monday	Jan.	October	Mar.
December	Sat.	Friday	Sept.
January	Mon.	November	Fri.

Rewrite the sentences. Write the complete words instead of the abbreviations.

Cindy goes to Vine St. for piano lessons every Mon., Wed., and Fri.

_____

_____

The coldest months in Michigan are Dec., Jan., and Feb.

_____

_____

 Review Work

Underline the nouns in the sentences with yellow.

 Draft Book

Write five sentences using nouns that name days and months. Write the abbreviations above the complete words.

▶ Make It Singular ⟩ singular and plural nouns

A noun can be singular (one person, place, thing, or idea) or plural (more than one). Usually, a noun becomes plural by adding an *s* to the end. Sometimes, a noun becomes singular by removing the *s* from the end.

Make the plural nouns singular. Use the nouns to finish the sentences. Decide if the plural or singular noun works best in each sentence.

turtles _____

   Kyra found (one) painted _____ .

   Vito found five box _____ .

bears _____

   Dan saw three baby _____ .

   Sydney saw an angry _____ .

ferrets _____

   Jennifer owns a brown _____ .

   The pet store has many _____ .

lizards _____

   Ian caught that _____ in a tree.

   He tried to catch other _____ , but they ran away.

Which words helped you decide whether you needed a singular or plural noun in each sentence? Circle the words that helped you. The first one has been done for you.

🔍 Review Work

Underline the other nouns in the sentences with yellow.

✏️ Draft Book

Write a paragraph about your favorite animal. Underline all of the nouns in the paragraph with yellow. Circle any plural nouns.

▶ Sports

▶ plural nouns

A noun can be singular (one person, place, thing, or idea) or plural (more than one). Usually, a noun becomes plural by adding an *s* to the end.

Make the nouns plural.

skate _____

base _____

hurdle _____

helmet _____

club _____

racket _____

guard _____

uniform _____

Use the plural nouns to finish the sentences.

Jackie and Mario need their _____ to play tennis.

Delaney needs shin _____ to play soccer.

Bobby got new hockey _____ for his birthday.

The team's softball _____ are blue.

The football players' _____ protected their heads.

Ling ran the _____ after she hit a home run.

Willie wants his own set of golf _____ .

Brian jumped over the _____ during track practice.

🔍 **Review Work**

Underline the other nouns in the sentences with yellow.

✏️ **Draft Book**

Write a paragraph about your favorite sport. Underline all of the nouns in the paragraph with yellow.

Name _____

▶ Critters

plural nouns

A noun can be singular (one person, place, thing, or idea) or plural (more than one).
Sometimes, a noun becomes plural by adding *es* to the end.

example: crutch ⟶ crutches   **example:** class ⟶ classes
example: dish ⟶ dishes   **example:** box ⟶ boxes

Make the nouns plural.

lunch _____   dash _____

pouch _____   crunch _____

dress _____   brush _____

finch _____   tax _____

fox _____   branch _____

Use some of the plural nouns to finish the sentences.

My dad packed _____ for my brother and me.

There are three _____ on the bathroom counter.

Kangaroos, opossums, and koalas use their _____ to carry
their young.

The _____ of the tree were filled with

_____ building nests.

🔍 Review Work

Underline the other nouns in the sentences with yellow.

✏️ Draft Book

Make a list of nouns that become plural by adding
es to the end of each. Start with the words on this page. Write the singular
and plural forms of the words. Use these nouns in future writings.

16 CD-4338 Grammar Rules! Grades 3–4

© Carson-Dellosa

Name _____

▶ Different Endings ▷ plural nouns

A noun can be singular (one person, place, thing, or idea) or plural (more than one). Usually, a noun becomes plural by adding an *s* to the end. A noun that ends with *ch*, *s*, *z*, *sh*, or *x* becomes plural by adding *es* to the end. A noun that ends with *f* or *fe* becomes plural by changing the *f* or *fe* to *v* and adding *es* to the end.

example: calf ⟶ cal**ves**   **example:** scarf ⟶ scar**ves**

Make the nouns plural.

leaf _____   coach _____

half _____   knife _____

bench _____   bunch _____

glass _____   lunch _____

Write the other form of each noun.

Red, yellow, and orange _____ are falling from the trees.
                                    leaf

Please put the _____ , _____ ,
                        dish   glass

_____ , and _____ on the table.
        knife   fork

For _____ , Jenna had two _____ of
        lunches   half

a sandwich and a _____ of _____ .
                        bunches   grape

🔍 **Review Work**

Draw a star above each singular noun in the sentences.

✏️ **Draft Book**

Two of the plural nouns were not used in the sentences. Write a sentence with each word. Underline the nouns with yellow.

Name _____

Here Come the Ys
plural nouns

A noun can be singular (one person, place, thing, or idea) or plural (more than one). There are two rules for making a noun that ends with *y* plural. For a noun that ends with a consonant + *y*, change the *y* to *i* and add *es* to the end. For a noun that ends with a vowel + *y*, add an *s* to the end.

example: lady → ladies   example: toy → toys

Make the nouns plural.

Tonya has seventeen _____ in her aquarium.

guppy

Did you forget your house _____ again?

key

Sometimes raccoons climb into _____ to make nests.

chimney

How many _____ do you have in your bank?

penny

Wild _____ live in the woods by Jon's house.

turkey

Hal loves to have _____ on his ice cream.

strawberry

Gerald has read many _____ about

story

_____ living in the rain forests.

monkey

 Review Work

Underline the other nouns in the sentences with yellow. Draw a star above each singular noun.

 Draft Book

Make these nouns plural: baby, pony, boy, and cherry. Use the plural nouns to write four sentences. Circle the plural nouns. Draw a star above each singular noun.

Name _____

▶ Make Mine Plural

A noun can be singular (one person, place, thing, or idea) or plural (more than one).
Make the nouns plural.

mess	_____	hobby	_____
wish	_____	thief	_____
wife	_____	donkey	_____
peach	_____	daisy	_____
dog	_____	mass	_____
way	_____	rash	_____
berry	_____	ray	_____
life	_____	baby	_____
crash	_____	sky	_____
toy	_____	watch	_____
shelf	_____	bay	_____
class	_____	candy	_____
elf	_____	day	_____

 Review Work

Write each singular noun from above that ends with *y* but does not have *es*
when it becomes plural.

_____

_____

 Draft Book

Choose five pairs of nouns (a pair includes both singular and plural forms).
Write a sentence with each noun.

▶ Tricky Nouns ▶ irregular plural nouns

A noun can be singular (one person, place, thing, or idea) or plural (more than one). Some nouns become plural by changing the middles or the ends.

example: goose ⟶ geese   **example:** mouse ⟶ mice

Some nouns do not change when they become plural.

examples: bison, buffalo, deer, fish, moose, series, sheep, swine

Draw lines to match the singular and plural nouns.

ox	feet
tooth	octopuses or octopi
child	men
foot	buses
person	children
octopus	people
man	oxen
woman	women
bus	teeth

Circle the tricky nouns in the sentences.

The children took buses to the aquarium to see water creatures like octopuses.

All people should brush their teeth twice daily.

Animals like deer and sheep are at the petting zoo.

Men lined up for tickets to the two series of playoffs.

The women rubbed their feet after running the race.

Review Work

Underline the other nouns in the sentences with yellow.

Draft Book

Write a story using some of the tricky nouns on this page. Underline the nouns with yellow. Circle the plural nouns. Draw a star above each singular noun.

Name _____

Mine, All Mine
> **possessive nouns**

A possessive noun shows belonging. If a noun is singular or if it is plural but does not end with an *s*, add an apostrophe + *s* (*'s*) to the end to make it possessive.
> **examples:** cat's food, boss's pen, men's shoes

If a noun is plural and already ends with an *s*, add an apostrophe to the end.
> **examples:** cats' collars, players' helmets

Finish each sentence with a possessive noun.

The pond belongs to those frogs. It is the _____ pond.

The crayons belong to Margaret. They are _____ crayons.

The bats belong to those boys. They are the _____ bats.

The swing belongs to Morris. It is _____ swing.

The hill belongs to the ants. It is the _____ hill.

The hat belongs to Max. It is _____ hat.

Those marbles belong to Louis. They are _____ marbles.

Make the nouns possessive.

girls _____   Chris _____

frog _____   Jordan _____

dogs _____   classmates _____

women _____   Mr. Moss _____

Tito _____   birds _____

teachers _____   turtle _____

 Review Work

Draw a star above each singular noun in the sentences. Circle the plural nouns.

 Draft Book

Write ten sentences with possessive nouns. Use both singular and plural nouns. Underline the nouns with yellow.

▶ Who Owns It? ▶ possessive nouns

A possessive noun shows belonging. If a noun is singular or if it is plural but does not end with an *s*, add an apostrophe + *s* ('*s*) to the end to make it possessive.

examples: cat's food, boss's pen, men's shoes

If a noun is plural and already ends with an *s*, add an apostrophe to the end.

examples: cats' collars, players' helmets

Circle the possessive noun in each sentence. How many people or things possess something? Circle 1 if one person or thing possesses something. Circle 2+ if more than one person or thing possesses something.

1	2+	The audience laughed at the comedian's performance.
1	2+	The turtles' pond needs a log in it.
1	2+	The dancer's shoes had holes in them.
1	2+	A book's pages must be treated gently.
1	2+	The chipmunks' home is stuffed with bird seed.
1	2+	Can you sharpen the students' pencils?
1	2+	The museum's admission price is $3.00.
1	2+	Liz let Craig's five birds out of their cages.
1	2+	The bluebird's nest has three eggs.
1	2+	Hakim borrowed the team's score book.
1	2+	Sandra washed her parents' cars.
1	2+	Omar's cat scratched me.

🔍 Review Work

Underline the other nouns in the sentences with yellow.

✏️ Draft Book

Choose four friends. Use possessive nouns to write sentences about things that belong to them. Write two sentences about each friend.

© Carson-Dellosa

▶ Hide-and-Seek

action verbs

An action verb tells what someone or something is doing.
    example: The boy **swings** the golf club.
    example: The mouse **scampers** across the floor.

Circle each action verb.

Waldo hides from his friend.

Marshall searches for the others.

Jane crouches behind the slide.

Sam crawls along the fence.

Sal jumps over the log.

Insects scatter out of the way.

Evelyn giggles behind the oak tree.

Joey climbs up the old maple.

The leaves on the old maple sway in the breeze.

Marshall finds Karen.

Karen races to the free spot.

Marshall tags Karen.

Karen yells for everyone to come out.

🔍 Review Work

Underline the nouns in the sentences with yellow.

✏️ Draft Book

Find a page in your draft book with the nouns underlined with yellow. Underline the verbs with blue.

Name _____

▶ Thunderstorm   action verbs

An action verb tells what someone or something is doing.

Use the verbs to finish the sentences. Use each verb only once.

whips	flashes	observes	pound
scurries	booms	crash	shine
slap	race	reports	hide

Jason _____ the storm from his bedroom window.

The meteorologist _____ the arrival of the storm.

Storm clouds _____ across the sky.

Lightning _____ in the distance.

Thunder _____ loudly.

Raindrops _____ the rooftops.

Joelynn _____ to find candles.

Wet branches _____ the windowpanes.

Stars _____ unseen behind the clouds.

The waves _____ against the shore.

The puppies _____ under the couch.

The wind _____ the waves into whitecaps.

🔍 Review Work

Draw a star above each singular noun in the sentences.
Circle the plural nouns.

✏️ Draft Book

Find a page in your draft book with the nouns underlined
with yellow. Underline the verbs with blue.

Name _____

▶ Entomologist

Linking verbs are verbs that do not show action. They express a state of being (to be). A linking verb connects, or links, two parts of a sentence.

Most linking verbs are forms of *to be*. There are eight forms of the verb *to be*: *am, are, is, was, were,* (*will*) *be,* (*am, are, was, were*) *being,* (*have, has, had*) *been.*

example: I **am** left-handed.   **example:** He **is** an artist.
example: You **are** a gymnast.   **example:** We **are** best friends.

Circle the linking verbs in the sentences.

I am an entomologist. An entomologist studies insects.

Insects are the most plentiful creatures on Earth.

A camera with a macro lens is an entomologist's tool.

A honeycomb cell is a home for one honeybee egg.

Larvae are baby insects that have hatched from eggs.

Monarchs are migrating butterflies.

A bee is a flying insect that can sting you.

A moth is different than a butterfly.

All ladybugs are not female.

Spiders are not insects. They are arachnids.

A pupa is the stage between larva and adult.

Who knew there was so much to learn about insects?

🔍 Review Work

Underline the common nouns in the sentences.

✏️ Draft Book

Write eight sentences that use linking verbs.
Underline the linking verbs with blue.

CD-4338 Grammar Rules! Grades 3–4   **25**

▶ Link Them Together ▶ linking verbs

Linking verbs are verbs that do not show action. They express a state of being. A linking verb connects, or links, two parts of a sentence. In a sentence, a linking verb comes before a noun or adjective—not an action verb.

Most linking verbs are forms of *to be*. There are eight forms of the verb *to be*: *am, are, is, was, were,* (*will*) *be,* (*am, are, was, were*) *being,* (*have, has, had*) *been.*

Circle the linking verbs in the sentences.

Rena was in the gym.

The garbage cans were full.

Hannah will be in second grade next year.

We have been patient.

Shane and James had been sick with the flu.

Those gray birds in that tree are being very noisy.

The picture above the door is one that I painted.

Matches are dangerous.

I am being careful near the baby.

Carol's hair is very short.

Richard has been asleep all afternoon.

The dinosaur fossils were very interesting.

 Review Work

Underline the common nouns in the sentences. Draw an X next to each proper noun that names a person. Draw a check next to the possessive noun.

✏️ **Draft Book**

Write eight sentences that use linking verbs. Use a variety of the verbs from this page. Underline the linking verbs with blue.

Name _____

▶ Artwork

Linking verbs are verbs that do not show action. They express a state of being. A linking verb connects, or links, two parts of a sentence. In a sentence, a linking verb comes before a noun or adjective—not an action verb.

Most linking verbs are forms of *to be*. There are eight forms of the verb *to be*: *am, are, is, was, were,* (*will*) *be,* (*am, are, was, were*) *being,* (*have, has, had*) *been.* Other linking verbs include forms of these verbs: *to appear, to become, to feel, to grow, to look, to remain, to seem, to smell, to sound, to taste.*

Circle the linking verbs in the sentences.

The art projects will remain in the classroom.

The pots in the kiln became too hot to touch.

The clay appeared hard, but it was really soft.

The molded bird with two heads looks unusual.

Randy sanded the wood table until it felt smooth.

Those ceramic wind chimes sound beautiful.

This glaze seems dry.

Many students become fans of art.

Those markers smell awful.

All of this artwork looks great!

Jake looks happy when he's painting.

 Review Work

Underline the nouns with yellow.

 Draft Book

Write 10 sentences that use linking verbs. Use a variety of the verbs from this page. Underline the linking verbs with blue.

Name _____

Lend a Hand

helping verbs

Helping verbs are verbs that help main verbs express tenses. There are 23 helping verbs. *Would, should, shall,* and *will* are helping verbs. Forms of the following verbs are also helping verbs:

be:	am, are, is, was, were, be, being, been
do:	do, does, did
have:	have, has, had
may:	may, must, might
can:	can, could

Circle the helping verb in each sentence. Draw an arrow to the verb it is helping.

That area under the trees would make a good picnic spot.

Those crickets are making a lot of noise.

Melissa has eaten her sandwich already.

Quinn might buy a new bike.

Halle is sneezing.

Ellie can chop nuts for the banana bread.

Matthew could answer that question for you.

Hunter's kitten had shredded the magazine.

Geno should rake the leaves this weekend.

Abby was coughing all night.

 Review Work

Underline the nouns in the sentences with yellow.

 Draft Book

Write five sentences with helping verbs. In each sentence, underline the helping verb and the verb being helped with blue.

Name _____

▶ Lots of Help

Helping verbs are verbs that help main verbs express tenses. There are 23 helping verbs. *Would, should, shall,* and *will* are helping verbs. Forms of the following verbs are also helping verbs:

        be: am, are, is, was, were, be, being, been
        do: do, does, did
        have: have, has, had
        may: may, must, might
        can: can, could

Up to three helping verbs can be used at one time.

    example: Annette **was** crying.
    example: Pete **should have** cut the grass.
    example: Dottie **will have been** sleeping for an hour when you finish.

Circle the helping verb(s) in each sentence. Draw an arrow to the verb being helped.

The cactus wrens in that old saguaro cactus are protected from predators.

The clay tiles are being mounted behind the sink in the kitchen.

Those fern fossils may have been found in sedimentary rocks.

Toothbrushes should be changed every two to three months.

Becky and Irene will be sleeping in that tent.

The red squirrel could have been hit by that car.

Nick and Luke were picking strawberries.

We may be going to the beach.

That huge oak tree must have fallen during the storm.

Review Work

Underline the nouns in the sentences with yellow.

Draft Book

Write eight sentences with helping verbs. In each sentence, underline the helping verb(s) and the verb being helped with blue.

Name _____

▶ You're Helping   helping verbs

Helping verbs are verbs that help main verbs express tenses. There are 23 helping verbs. *Would*, *should*, *shall*, and *will* are helping verbs. Forms of the following verbs are also helping verbs:

be: am, are, is, was, were, be, being, been
do: do, does, did
have: have, has, had
may: may, must, might
can: can, could

Up to three helping verbs can be used at one time.

example: Tina **is** practicing her dance routine.
example: Oliver **could be** hiding behind the gazebo.
example: Tyler **would have been** hiking if he hadn't gotten sick.

Finish the sentences with helping verbs. Use a different helping verb or helping verb combination in each sentence.

Those goldfish _____ swimming through the water.

The trailer _____ attached to the trailer hitch.

Perry _____ go to the movie.

Caleb _____ ride his scooter.

Ned _____ clear the table.

Dylan _____ baking cookies.

The boys _____ racing their toy cars.

Keesha _____ turned on the light.

 Review Work

In the sentences, draw an arrow from the helping verb(s) to the verb being helped.

 Draft Book

Write 10 sentences with helping verbs. In each sentence, underline the helping verb(s) and the verb being helped with blue.

© Carson-Dellosa

Name _____

▶ Now and Then

Verbs use tenses to tell when something is happening. When the action happens now, it is present tense. When the action happened in the past, it is past tense. One way to make a verb past tense is to add *ed* to the end.

example: Sam **studies** for the test. (present tense)
example: Sam **studied** for the test. (past tense)

Circle the verb in each sentence. Write whether the verb is past tense or present tense.

The sea horse floats by the starfish. _____

The paper's color faded in the sunlight. _____

The string tangled into a huge knot. _____

Neil disturbed the sleeping puppy. _____

The kites dance in the breeze. _____

Sean sharpens his pencil. _____

Noelle bandaged her finger. _____

Children tumble down the sand dune. _____

Cameron flicked the paper football. _____

Walter defends his snow fort. _____

Review Work

Underline the nouns in the sentences with yellow.

Draft Book

Choose five of the sentences. If the verb is present tense, rewrite it in the past tense. If the verb is past tense, rewrite it in the present tense.

Name _____

▶ At the Zoo

Verbs use tenses to tell when something is happening. When the action happens now, it is present tense. When the action happened in the past, it is past tense. One way to make a verb past tense is to add *ed* to the end.

Underline the present tense verb in the first sentence. Add *ed* to make the verb past tense in the second sentence.

The koalas munch on eucalyptus leaves.

They _____ on the leaves before they napped.

Prairie dogs burrow in the dirt.

Yesterday, they _____ for hours.

The owls rest in the shade.

They _____ in the shade last summer.

Piranhas pounce on their food.

They _____ on their food yesterday, too.

The monkeys screech at the visitors.

They _____ at the visitors, then went to play.

Lions pace in their cage.

They _____ in their cage all afternoon.

Crocodiles drift just below the water.

They _____ toward their feeding area an hour ago.

◯ Review Work

Underline the nouns in the sentences with yellow.

✏ Draft Book

Find a story you wrote in your Draft Book. Draw a box around each verb with an *ed* ending.

Name _____

▶ Pick the Right Verb ▶ past and present tense

Verbs use tenses to tell when something is happening. When the action happens now, it is present tense. When the action happened in the past, it is past tense. One way to make a verb past tense is to add *ed* to the end.

example: Amy **hugs** her baby sister. (present tense)
example: Amy **hugged** her baby sister. (past tense)

Circle the correct verb in each sentence.

Don't (play, played) with your pencil.

The boxers (punch, punched) the punching bags before they stepped in the ring.

Heidi (slumps, slumped) in her chair when she heard about the quiz.

Jill washes the windows, and Jared (mops, mopped) the floor.

Milo (hunts, hunted) for his homework when the teacher asked for it.

I like to watch boats (cruise, cruised) through that channel.

Last week, Holly and Eddie (hike, hiked) in Pratt Park.

Patrick was grounded because he (teases, teased) his sister.

Iris and Lavonia (soak, soaked) in the hot tub last night.

James watches the movie, but Randy (snoozes, snoozed) through it.

 Review Work

Underline the word or words that helped you decide whether each sentence needed a present or past tense verb.

 Draft Book

Write a story using verbs with *ed* endings. Draw a box around each past tense verb.

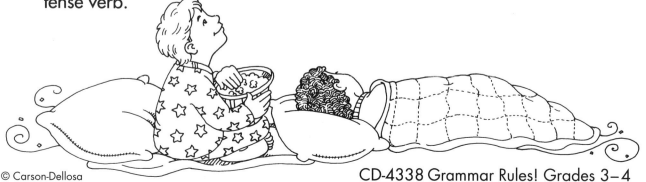

▶ Telling Time

past tense

Verb tenses tell when something is happening. When the action happens now, it is present tense. When the action happened in the past, it is past tense. There are several ways to add *ed* to a verb to make it past tense.

Most verbs add *ed* or *d* to the ends of the base words.

example: box + ed = boxed   **example:** wave + d = waved

If a verb ends with a consonant + *y*, change *y* to *i* and add *ed* to the end.

example: carry + ed = carried   **example:** bury + ed = buried

If a verb ends with a short vowel + one consonant, double the consonant and add *ed* to the end.

example: tip + ed = tipped   **example:** stop + ed = stopped

Change these verbs to the past tense.

breathe	chip	hurry
_____	_____	_____
cruise	tap	dry
_____	_____	_____
parachute	toast	play
_____	_____	_____
trip	comb	copy
_____	_____	_____
shop	try	pounce
_____	_____	_____

 Review Work

Choose one of the verbs. Use it to write a sentence.

_____

 Draft Book

Choose five verbs. Write two sentences for each verb, using the present tense of the verb in one sentence and the past tense in the other sentence.

Name _____

▶ Busy, Busy past tense

Verb tenses tell when something is happening. When the action happens now, it is present tense. When the action happened in the past, it is past tense. There are several ways to add *ed* to a verb to make it past tense.

Most verbs add *ed* or *d* to the ends of the base words.

example: box + ed = boxed   **example:** wave + d = waved

If a verb ends with a consonant + *y*, change *y* to *i* and add *ed* to the end.

example: carry + ed = carried   **example:** bury + ed = buried

If a verb ends with a short vowel + one consonant, double the consonant and add *ed* to the end.

example: tip + ed = tipped   **example:** stop + ed = stopped

Make the verbs past tense to finish the sentences.

study   Diane _____ the bud with a magnifying glass.

copy   George _____ his partner's actions.

trim   Nigel _____ the cat's claws.

rake   Dakota _____ the leaves.

skip   Mallory _____ down the hall.

chop   Kevin _____ onions and peppers for pizza.

frame   Libby _____ the class photo.

grab   Josie _____ the dog's leash.

empty   Cole _____ the aquarium.

whine   Peanut _____ for her bone.

🔍 Review Work

Underline the nouns in the sentences with yellow.

✏️ Draft Book

Write six sentences using verbs in the past tense.

Name _____

▶ Tricky Verbs

Verb tenses tell when something is happening. When the action happens now, it is present tense. When the action happened in the past, it is past tense. One way to make a verb past tense is to add *ed* to the end. An irregular verb becomes past tense by changing its spelling.

example: Brian **rings** the bell. (present tense)
example: Brian **rang** the bell. (past tense)

example: Rose **swims** across the pool. (present tense)
example: Rose **swam** across the pool. (past tense)

Write the past tense of the irregular verbs to finish the sentences.

Georgia _____ (tell) us about the book she read.

Andy _____ (take) the last cookie.

Tyra _____ (run) around the bases.

Grady _____ (give) me his spot in line.

Victor _____ (come) to school late.

Leon _____ (sing) in the choir.

Joan _____ (meet) the new principal.

Emily _____ (begin) to work hard.

Darren _____ (know) how to fix the sharpener.

William _____ (leave) his soccer cleats at home.

Fernando _____ (write) a great poem.

Judy _____ (sit) on the new couch.

 Review Work

Underline the nouns in the sentences with yellow.

 Draft Book

Choose five irregular verbs from this page. Write one sentence using the present tense and one sentence using the past tense of each verb.

Name _____

▶ More Tricky Verbs ▶ past tense

Verb tenses tell when something is happening. When the action happens now, it is present tense. When the action happened in the past, it is past tense. One way to make a verb past tense is to add *ed* to the end. An irregular verb becomes past tense by changing its spelling.

examples: bite / bit   bring / brought   drink / drank

Write the past tense of the irregular verbs to finish the sentences.

Mrs. Walker _____ me to understand fractions.
teaches

Grandpa _____ a bunch of fish.
catches

The elephant _____ the chain.
breaks

Many monkeys _____ through the trees.
swing

The kickball players _____ teams during recess.
choose

The children _____ down the hill on a sled.
slide

Katie _____ the ball to Hope.
throws

The allergy shot _____ for just a minute.
stings

Brad _____ up when his alarm clock rang.
wakes

🔍 Review Work
Underline the nouns with yellow.

✏️ Draft Book
Write your own past tense sentence with each irregular verb from this page. Underline the verbs with blue.

Name _____

▶ Under the Sea ▶ future tense

Verb tenses tell when something is happening. When the action is going to happen in the future, it is future tense. The helping verb *will* is added before the main verb to make the future tense. If the noun is singular, the *s* is dropped before adding *will*.

example: Dad **mows** the lawn. (present)
example: Dad **will mow** the lawn. (future)

Underline the present tense verb in the first sentence.
Rewrite the sentence in the future tense.

present tense: Sharks swim through the water.

future tense: _____

present tense: Jellyfish float on the currents.

future tense: _____

present tense: Manta rays sail through the water.

future tense: _____

present tense: Sea slugs meander along the bottom.

future tense: _____

present tense: Anemones prey on unwary fish.

future tense: _____

present tense: Octopuses squirt ink.

future tense: _____

🔍 Review Work

Write the past tense of each verb from the sentences.

Draft Book

Write five sentences using verbs in the future tense. Put the helping word *will* in front of each verb. Underline the verbs with blue, including the word *will*.

Which Is Correct?

past and future tense

Verb tenses tell when something is happening. When the action is going to happen in the future, it is future tense. The helping verb *will* is added before the main verb to make the future tense. If the noun is singular, the *s* is dropped before adding *will*.

example: Charlotte **eats** the cake. (present)

example: Charlotte **will eat** the cake. (future)

Circle the correct verb in each sentence.

I (complete, will complete) my homework tonight.

Barry already (filled, will fill) the pails with sand to make a castle.

Carmen's parents (tried, will try) to contact her coach tomorrow.

Julie (ate, will eat) pizza for lunch yesterday.

Mr. Zeer (draw, will draw) plans for a new house this summer.

Briana (began, will begin) work on her project last Thursday.

Next week, Stephen and John (hiked, will hike) on the trail.

Matt (watches, will watch) the movie next Friday.

Last year, it (rained, will rain) during our family vacation.

Misty (open, will open) presents on her birthday.

 Review Work

Underline the word or words that helped you decide whether each sentence needed a past or future tense verb.

 Draft Book

Write your own sentence with each future tense verb from this page.

Name _____

Verb tenses tell when something is happening. When the action is going to happen in the future, it is future tense. The helping verb *will* is added before the main verb to make the future tense. If the noun is singular, the *s* is dropped before adding *will*.

    example: Bob **raked** the lawn. (past)
    example: Bob **will rake** the lawn. (future)

Write the correct future tense verb on the line.

Ian has plans to go into space.

A group (built) _____ a huge rocket.

Technicians (checked) _____ safety issues.

Ian and his dad (mapped) _____ the journey
ahead of time.

Ian and his friends (boarded) _____ the rocket.

The announcer (counted) _____ down to zero.

The rocket (exploded) _____ into orbit.

The crew (viewed) _____ Earth from space.

They (observed) _____ comets and asteroids.

Ian (kept) _____ a day-to-day journal.

Marshall (recorded) _____ space sounds.

Emily (photographed) _____ interesting things.

Jennifer (collected) _____ space dust.

They (returned) _____ to Earth with many photos,
recordings, items, and stories.

 Review Work

    Underline the nouns with yellow.

✏️ **Draft Book**

    Write about your own imaginary trip using future tense.

Name _____

Verb tenses tell when something is happening.

Underline the verbs in the sentences. If the verb is future tense, underline both the main verb and the helping verb *will*. Circle past, present, or future.

Vanessa signed her name on the card.	past	present	future
Greg will golf in the tournament.	past	present	future
Maegen snaps the links together.	past	present	future
Brantley climbs into his bunk bed.	past	present	future
Layne will set her alarm clock.	past	present	future
Kallie rocked her puppy to sleep.	past	present	future
Jill will dip the strawberries in chocolate.	past	present	future
Raymond catches a line drive.	past	present	future
Jade calculated the answer.	past	present	future
Fran will input the test.	past	present	future
Lisa will prepare lunch.	past	present	future
Ryan pestered his mother.	past	present	future
Lori sealed the envelope.	past	present	future
Teresa will polish her fingernails.	past	present	future
Mike will spend the night at a friend's house.	past	present	future

 Review Work

Underline the nouns with yellow.

 Draft Book

Write two sentences for each verb tense. Underline the verbs with blue.
Label the sentences past tense, present tense, or future tense.

Name _____

▶ Not, Not, Not!

A contraction is two words that are put together to form one word. Some of the letters drop out of the second word when the words are joined. An apostrophe replaces those letters.

The word *not* forms a contraction with many helping or linking verbs.

    example: did + not = didn't

The contraction for *will not* is an exception: will + not = won't.

Add *n't* to the helping or linking verbs to make contractions.

are _____   is _____

was _____   were _____

do _____   does _____

can _____   had _____

has _____   should _____

Write a contraction for each sentence. Try to use each contraction only once.

Sharon and Jill _____ follow the directions.

Gerard _____ canoe without a life jacket.

Antoine _____ know how to cook.

Madalen _____ very hungry.

Caleb _____ phoned me yet.

Maegen _____ tired.

Mia _____ cleaned the horse stall when I left.

🔍 **Review Work**

Find the other verbs in the sentences. Underline them with blue.

✏️ **Draft Book**

Choose six contractions. Write a sentence with each one.

Name _____

▶ Throw Some Out ▸ contractions

A contraction is two words that are put together to form one word. Some of the letters drop out of the second word when the words are joined. An apostrophe replaces those letters. The following letters are left with the apostrophe when a contraction is made:

n't when you add *not* (isn**'t**)   **'ll** when you add *will* (she**'ll**)
'd when you add *would* or *had* (we**'d**)   **'s** when you add *is* or *has* (it**'s**)
're when you add *are* (we**'re**)   **'ve** when you add *have* (I**'ve**)

Combine the words to make contractions.

I + will = _____   he + is = _____

they + are = _____   they + have = _____

he + will = _____   she + has = _____

I + had = _____   they + would = _____

what + is = _____   here + is = _____

could + not = _____   they + will = _____

Write the correct contraction on the line in each sentence.

Carter **should not** _____ ride his skateboard without a helmet.

Ariel **did not** _____ remember to do her homework.

That is the strangest thing **I have** _____ ever seen!

Do you think **they are** _____ coming to the game?

I think **I will** _____ buy a new backpack.

Who is _____ on the telephone?

🔍 **Review Work**

Underline the action verbs in the sentences with blue.

✏️ **Draft Book**

Choose eight contractions. Write a sentence with each one.

▶ What We're Doing ▶ verb endings

A verb follows the same rules as a noun when adding *s* or *es* to the end.

Add *s* to the ends of most verbs.

Add *es* to the end if the verb ends with *sh, s, z, ch,* or *x.*

Change *y* to *i* and add *es* to the end if the verb ends with a consonant + *y.*

Add *s* to the end if the verb ends with a vowel + *y.*

example: run + s = runs

example: pitch + es = pitches

example: try + es = tries

example: enjoy + s = enjoys

Finish each sentence with the verb and its correct ending.

crunch   Anna _____ on a carrot.

fly   Amelia _____ her kite.

toy   Cody _____ with his food.

fix   Nell _____ her bicycle.

dish   Ben _____ out the spaghetti.

play   Vinny _____ the piano.

buzz   Paul _____ like a bee.

teach   Maria _____ her brother to tie his shoes.

finish   Frank _____ his ice cream.

pass   Ronald _____ the football.

spy   Wrenn _____ on her friends.

🔍 Review Work

What kind of verb is used in each sentence?
Circle the correct answer.

action   linking   helping

✏️ Draft Book

Write five sentences. Use singular nouns and verbs with the correct endings.
Use the rules on this page.

▶ Twilight

noun and verb agreement

A singular noun uses a verb that has an *s* at the end.
> **example:** The boy **climbs** the tree.

A plural noun uses a verb that does not have an *s* at the end.
> **example:** The boys **climb** the tree.

Circle the correct verb(s) in each sentence.

Fluffy white clouds (drift, drifts) along.

The sun (fade, fades) behind the horizon.

A dog (bound, bounds) into the yard.

The door (open, opens).

The boy (hear, hears) many sounds.

Buddy (run, runs) into the woods and Calvin (follow, follows).

Calvin (walk, walks) out after his dog, Buddy.

Owls (call, calls) to one another.

Insects (buzz, buzzes) and (hum, hums).

Bullfrogs (croak, croaks).

The two friends (return, returns) home in soft darkness.

Stars (twinkle, twinkles) in the sky.

Calvin (call, calls) quietly to Buddy.

Buddy (reenter, reenters) the house with Calvin.

🔍 Review Work

Underline the nouns in the sentences with yellow.

✏️ Draft Book

Choose five of the sentences. Rewrite each one so that the first noun becomes the opposite (singular or plural) of what it is now. Make sure the verb has the correct ending to agree with the new noun.

Name _____

A singular noun uses a verb that has an *s* at the end.

    example: The girl **runs** in the race.

A plural noun uses a verb that does not have an *s* at the end.

    example: The girls **run** in the race.

Use some of the verbs to finish the sentences. Add an *s* to the end of each verb if it is needed. Use each verb only once.

balance	bounce	climb	flip	sit	race	jump
hit	pitch	shoot	leap	roll	tie	lie

The girls _____ their shoes for a walk.

Quincy _____ the baseball to the batter.

Laura _____ the ball with the bat.

Kayleigh _____ the rope.

Rob _____ the basketball.

The basketball players _____ baskets.

The runners _____ to the finish line.

Abe _____ over the hurdles.

Kit _____ on the beam.

Justin's classmates _____ on the mat for sit-ups.

Ginger _____ off the bars.

Zane's friends _____ down the hill.

🔍 Review Work

Underline the common nouns in the sentences. Draw an X next to each proper noun that names a person.

✏️ Draft Book

Write eight sentences using both singular and plural nouns. Make sure the verbs have the correct endings to agree with the nouns.

© Carson-Dellosa

▶ Five Senses

noun and verb agreement

A singular noun uses a verb that has an *s* at the end. A plural noun uses a verb that does not have an *s* at the end.

Choose the correct noun and verb to finish each sentence. Write the words on the lines.

The horse's _____ _____ the apple.
tooth / teeth   chomps / chomp

Sal's right _____ _____ better than his left eye.
eye / eyes   see / sees

Paul's left _____ _____ when he doesn't believe you.
eyebrow / eyebrows   lift / lifts

A rabbit's two long _____ can _____ a fox coming.
ear / ears   hear / hears

My _____ _____ something good.
nose / noses   smells / smell

Our _____ can _____ freshly baked cookies.
mouth / mouths   taste / tastes

All of our _____ _____ in the sand.
toe / toes   wiggle / wiggles

The baby's five little _____ _____ her cheek.
finger / fingers   touches / touch

🔍 **Review Work**

Underline the singular nouns in the sentences with yellow.

✏️ **Draft Book**

Write a story. Underline the nouns in the story with yellow. Underline the verbs with blue. Make sure your nouns and verbs agree.

Name _____

▶ Describers

Adjectives are words that describe nouns. Adjectives tell what kind, how many, or which one. They can include number, color, size, shape, or other detail words.

example: The **dirty** puppy needs a bath.

example: The **public** library is closed today.

A sentence can have more than one adjective: **Four, gray** bugs are in the **small** garden.

Circle the adjectives. Draw an arrow from the adjective to the noun it describes.

An excited Devon opened the wrapped package.

Many tiny ants crawled across the jelly sandwich.

A bothersome mosquito buzzes near my ear.

The sweet, sticky cotton candy is gone.

Walter has dirty socks and muddy shoes in that bag.

Four spotted dalmatians rode on the noisy, red fire engine.

Sal used the sharp scissors to cut the thick, brown paper.

Justin squeezed two tart lemons for lemonade.

Polly ate a large, red apple.

Zoe listened to the jazz music.

○ Review Work

Underline the nouns with yellow and the verbs with blue.

✏ Draft Book

Write five sentences that have adjectives in them. Circle the adjectives. Draw an arrow from each adjective to the noun it describes.

Name _____

▶ Find and Circle

Adjectives are words that describe nouns. Circle the adjectives.

young	held	smooth	Anna	silver
know	eleven	damp	cranky	grandmother
purple	nasty	rotten	boots	shown
goofy	prickly	phone	chilly	tissue
speedy	ripped	tight	exhausted	Ohio
rectangular	dog	slept	pen	run

Add adjectives to finish the sentences. You may use adjectives from the word bank.

The _____ water was fun to swim in.

Mrs. Capsin carried a _____ basket.

The _____ owl hooted softly.

Jessie ate the _____ pie.

The _____ sand toasted our

_____ feet.

_____ children gathered for the

_____ program.

Emma touched the _____ cockroach.

The _____ snake slithered across the

_____ sidewalk.

 Review Work

In the word bank, underline the nouns with yellow and the verbs with blue.

 Draft Book

Write five sentences that have adjectives in them. Circle the adjectives. Draw an arrow from each adjective to the noun it describes.

Name _____

▶ Get the Picture

Adjectives are words that describe nouns. They tell what kind, how many, or which one.

Write three adjectives for each noun, one adjective for each category. Do not repeat any adjectives. The first one has been done for you.

noun	What kind?	How many?	Which one?
gorilla	furry	few	black
plant			
cookie			
mansion			
costume			
planet			
volcano			
insect			
lizard			

◯ Review Work

Choose two noun/adjective sets. Write a sentence using the words.

_____

_____

✎ Draft Book

Write a story using the other noun/adjective sets.
Underline the nouns with yellow. Circle each
adjective and draw an arrow to the noun
it describes.

Name _____

Nouns are words that name people, places, and things. Verbs are words that tell what someone or something is doing. Adjectives are words that describe nouns. Sometimes a word that is a noun in one sentence can be a verb or adjective in another sentence. How the word is used in a sentence determines what type of word it is.

example: That **fly** is bothering me. (noun)
example: I **fly** my kite. (verb)
example: Jamie caught the **fly** ball. (adjective)

What type of word is the underlined word in each sentence? Write adjective, noun, or verb on each line.

Sam will iron his <u>wrinkled</u> pants. _____

Jane <u>wrinkled</u> her nose at the nasty smell. _____

The <u>ship</u> is docked at the pier. _____

The Shoes Company will <u>ship</u> my new boots tomorrow. _____

Goldfish live in a <u>liquid</u> environment. _____

This <u>liquid</u> will pour easily. _____

Brad likes the <u>painted</u> horse best. _____

Fran <u>painted</u> her dresser blue. _____

Vin <u>paints</u> many things. _____

Katie bought a new set of <u>paints</u>. _____

 Review Work

Underline the verbs in the sentences with blue. Next to each sentence, write the verb tense: P = present, S = past, or F = future.

 Draft Book

Think of two words that can be used as a noun and a verb. Write two sentences for each of the words. Use the words differently in each sentence.

Name _____

At the Beginning

A prefix is a group of letters added to the beginning of a word. It adds meaning or changes word meaning. The word the prefix is added to is called the root, or base, word. When adding a prefix, the spelling of the root word is not changed.

Some common prefixes are *re-*, *un-*, *pre-*, *dis-*, *mis-*, *bi-*, and *uni-*.

re: again   **pre:** before   **un, dis, mis:** not or against   **bi:** two   **uni:** one

Match the words with their meanings.

unhappy	wind again
bicycle	not known
rewind	every two months
uncover	cycle with one wheel
uninformed	not happy
prewritten	not cover
bimonthly	not informed
unknown	cycle with two wheels
unicycle	written before

Underline the words with prefixes in each sentence. Write the meaning of the word on the line.

anabelle's umbrella remained unopened until it began to rain

_____

cicily bought prewashed jeans

_____

sam is going for his biweekly allergy shot

_____

 Review Work

Add uppercase letters and ending punctuation to the sentences.

 Draft Book

Make a list of words that use prefixes. Write the full word, then the prefix and base word separately. Use these words in future writing assignments.

Name _____

▶ At the End   suffixes -er and -est

A suffix is a group of letters added to the end of a word. It adds meaning or changes a word's meaning. The word the suffix is added to is called the root, or base, word. Most words just add endings; however, there are exceptions.

> If a word ends with *e*, drop the *e* and add the ending: make - e + er = maker
> If a word ends in *y*, change *y* to *i* and add the ending:
>   happy - y + i + er = happier
> If a word ends with a short vowel with one consonant, double the consonant and add the ending: fat + t + er = fatter

Two common suffixes are *-er* and *-est*. *-Er* means more. *-Est* means most. Sometimes when *-er* is added to a verb, however, it makes a noun that means *someone who*.
>   **example:** A **painter** is someone who paints.

Write the underlined base word with the correct ending.

The animal that is the most <u>mean</u> is the _____ .

The person who is the most <u>loud</u> is the _____ .

Someone who is more <u>fast</u> is _____ .

A person who <u>bakes</u> is a _____ .

The child who is more <u>quiet</u> is _____ .

A person who <u>swims</u> is a _____ .

The person who is the most <u>angry</u> is the _____ .

Underline the word with a suffix. Write its meaning on the line.

your sunglasses are darker than mine   _____

that is the slowest horse of the bunch   _____

that aisle is narrower than it was before   _____

🔍 Review Work

Add uppercase letters and add ending punctuation in the last three sentences.

✏️ Draft Book

Write ten sentences using words with the suffixes *-er* and *-est*.

▶ Endings  suffixes

A suffix is a group of letters added to the end of a word. It adds meaning or changes a word's meaning. The word the suffix is added to is called the root, or base, word. When a suffix begins with a vowel, a change to the base word may be needed.

If a word ends with *e*, drop the *e* and add the ending: bake - e + ing = baking

If a word ends in a consonant + *y*, change *y* to *i* and add the ending (if adding *-ing*, keep the *y* and add *-ing*): carry - y + i + ed = carried
hurry + ing = hurrying

If a word ends in a vowel + *y*, add the ending: play + ing = playing

If a word has a short vowel with one consonant, double the consonant and add the ending: sun + n + y = sunny   bat + t + ed = batted

Some common suffixes that begin with vowels are: *-ed, -ing, -able, -er, -y,* and *-est.*

Write the base word with the suffix.

love + able = _____   bike + er = _____

carry + ing = _____   nice + est = _____

stop + ed = _____   scurry + ed = _____

fun + y = _____   identify + ing = _____

Circle the correct spelling.

Olive is (carriing, carrying) a large box.

Ian (multiplyed, multiplied) the two numbers.

Jerome is (rideing, riding) his bike.

Flora watched that (scarey, scary) movie.

🔍 Review Work

Underline the nouns in the sentences with yellow.

✏️ Draft Book

Make a list of words that use suffixes. Write the full word, then the suffix and base word separately. Use these words in future writing assignments.

Name _____

▶ Endings

suffixes

A suffix is a group of letters added to the end of a word. It adds meaning or changes a word's meaning. The word the suffix is added to is called the root, or base, word. When a suffix begins with a consonant, changes to the base word are usually not needed.

Some common suffixes beginning with consonants are: *-ful*, *-ly*, *-less*, and *-ness*.

Write the base word with the suffix.

pain + ful = _____

forget + ful = _____

forgive + ness = _____

fear + ful + ly = _____

sincere + ly = _____

near + ly = _____

fear + less = _____

hair + less = _____

care + less = _____

grace + ful = _____

sad + ness = _____

glad + ness = _____

 Review Work

Write five sentences using words with suffixes. You may use some of the words listed above or choose your own.

 Draft Book

Find a page of writing in your Draft Book. Choose three words on the page that you can add suffixes to. Write the root words and the suffixes separately, then the full word. Tell what each new word means.

Name _____

How, Where, or When **adverbs**

Adverbs are words that tell more about verbs. They tell how, where, or when something happens.

Underline the verb in each sentence. Circle the adverbs that tell how, where, and when.

Janice closes the book quickly.

Tito frequently plays in the park.

Missie will watch that movie tonight.

Zack worked quietly on his model.

Leo ran on the bike path last week.

Pete and Susie flew to their grandma's yesterday.

Walter will miss his game tomorrow.

Tracy mixed the ingredients carefully.

Rick will eat strawberries later.

Ariel often stops to pick flowers.

 ### Review Work

Underline the nouns in the sentences with yellow.

 ### Draft Book

Write a story about your favorite movie. Include adverbs. Circle the adverbs with purple.

Name _____

▶ How Was It Done? ▶ adverbs

Adverbs are words that tell more about verbs. They tell how, where, or when something happens.

What does each adverb tell about the verb? Write *how*, *where*, or *when* on each line. Draw an arrow to the verb the adverb is telling more about.

Kylie worked **smarter** than she had in the past. _____

Neil swam **through** the channel. _____

Archie jogs **daily**. _____

The wind **wildly** blew the branches. _____

Rico complained **loudly**. _____

The storm will be here **soon**. _____

Jennifer **never** cheats. _____

Jade **cheerfully** sets the table. _____

Ian **always** wears his bike helmet. _____

Simon rubbed the wet dog **vigorously** with a towel. _____

After playing all day, Gwen went **inside** to relax. _____

Meg put the cookies **up** on the shelf. _____

 ### Review Work

Underline the nouns in the sentences with yellow.

 ### Draft Book

Write a story about a thunderstorm you remember. Include adverbs. Circle the adverbs with purple.

 # Tell About It

adverbs

Adverbs are words that tell more about verbs. They tell how, where, or when something happens.

Write three adverbs for each verb, one adverb for each category. Do not repeat any adverbs.

verb	How?	Where?	When?
climb	_____	_____	_____
exercise	_____	_____	_____
screech	_____	_____	_____
munch	_____	_____	_____
paint	_____	_____	_____
explode	_____	_____	_____
sting	_____	_____	_____
shred	_____	_____	_____

 ### Review Work

Choose two verb/adverbs sets. Write a sentence using each set of words. Change the tenses of the verbs if needed.

_____

_____

Draft Book

Write a story using the other verb/adverbs sets. Underline the verbs with blue. Circle each adverb with purple and draw an arrow to the verb it describes.

▶ Mathematics

articles a, an, the

A, *an*, and *the* are articles. An article comes before a noun or adjective/noun combination. Use *a* in front of words that start with a consonant sound. Use *an* in front of words that start with a vowel sound. Use *the* if reference is being made to a specific thing or things.

Write *a* or *an* in front of these mathematical items.

_____ intersection

_____ addend

_____ right triangle

_____ fraction

_____ equal sign

_____ difference

_____ ordered pair

_____ cone

_____ multiple

_____ addition problem

_____ subtraction symbol

_____ sum

_____ even number

_____ odd number

Write *a*, *an*, or *the* on the lines.

Lillie is learning about shapes in math. She draws _____ oval on her paper. _____ oval has no corners or sides. Next, she draws _____ octagon, which is _____ eight-sided figure. Then, Lillie draws _____ figure with _____ acute angle. Lillie enjoys drawing _____ different shapes. Now, she will color _____ shapes with _____ marker.

🔍 Review Work

Circle the uppercase letter at the beginning of each sentence and the ending punctuation.

✏️ Draft Book

Find a story you have written in your Draft Book. Circle the articles in orange. If an article is incorrect, fix it.

Name _____

▶ Pick the Pronoun > subject pronouns

A pronoun takes the place of a noun. Subject pronouns take the place of the simple subject nouns. They are: *I, you, he, she, we, they,* and *it.*

Above each group of words, write the pronoun that could replace each word in the group. Add four nouns to each list.

_____

helicopter _____
antelope _____
statue _____
computer _____

_____

my sister _____
Ms. Lee _____
Betsy _____
Grandma _____

_____

the kindergartners _____
Pete, Jan, and Leon _____
the crowd _____
that family _____

_____

my class and I _____
my sister and I _____
my team and I _____
you and I _____

_____

Dad _____
my brother _____
Mr. Nelson _____
Ned _____

🔍 **Review Work**

Draw an X next to each proper noun.

✏️ **Draft Book**

Write a story about your friends. Underline the subject pronouns with red.

© Carson-Dellosa

Name _____

▶ Who Did It?

subject pronouns

A pronoun takes the place of a noun. A subject pronoun usually comes before a verb. Subject pronouns take the place of the simple subject nouns. They are: *I*, *you*, *he*, *she*, *we*, *they*, and *it*.

Replace each noun in bold type with a subject pronoun. Write the correct pronoun on the line.

Dillon's sheep produced bags of wool. _____

Alexis and **Anika** live in Hong Kong. _____

Mr. Arc is my math teacher. _____

Jeremy dove into the pool. _____

My bike needs a new tire. _____

Mary won first prize. _____

The sun toasted my nose. _____

Judy caught an enormous fish. _____

Anna and I made a castle at the beach. _____

Write two sentences using the pronoun *you*.

_____

_____

Write two sentences using the pronoun *I*.

_____

_____

🔍 Review Work

Underline the nouns in the sentences with yellow.

✏️ Draft Book

Find a page of writing in your Draft Book. Change the subject nouns to subject pronouns.

Name _____

▶ Past the Verb   ▶ object pronouns

An object pronoun takes the place of a noun found in the complete predicate. An object pronoun usually comes after a verb. Object pronouns are: *me, you, her, him, them, us,* and *it.*

Replace each noun in bold type with an object pronoun. Write the correct pronoun on the line.

Fiona lobbed **the tennis ball** to Sarah.   _____

Gena and I told the secret to **David.**   _____

Dillon sent the package to **Blake and Hailey.**   _____

Mrs. Mars read the book with **Willie and me.**   _____

Spencer spoke on the phone with **Dan.**   _____

The basketball swished through **the hoop.**   _____

Sydney biked to the park with **Jessica.**   _____

Lars handed **the salt** to Timothy.   _____

The garbage truck knocked **the garbage cans** over.   _____

Alexis made a sand castle with **Reanne and me.**   _____

Write a sentence using the object pronoun *me* **and one with the object pronoun** *you.* **Remember to place each pronoun after the verb.**

   example: The bright sun gave me a headache.

_____

_____

 Review Work

   Underline the nouns with yellow. Write the correct subject pronouns above the nouns that are before the verbs.

 Draft Book

   Write a story about a book you read recently. Use subject and object pronouns in your story. Underline the pronouns with red.

▶ I or Me?

pronouns

Pronouns take the place of nouns. Subject pronouns take the place of subject nouns. Object pronouns take the place of predicate nouns. A subject pronoun usually comes before a verb. An object pronoun usually comes after a verb.

> subject pronouns: I, you, he, she, we, they, it
> object pronouns: me, you, her, him, them, us, it

Circle the correct pronoun.

(I, Me) went to the library.

Can you come to the pool with (we, us)?

(He, Him) helped (I, me) put up the poster.

Hannah delivered the package to (they, them).

(She, Her) caught a butterfly.

(We, Us) will build a tree fort.

Did (he, him) get a turn?

Joe threw the ball to (he, him).

Karen likes soccer, but (she, her) likes golf better.

Mr. Paulson checked out the book to (she, her).

(She, Her) will put the stamp on the envelope. Then, (she, her) will mail it.

(We, Us) went with (she, her) to the store.

 Review Work

Draw a X next to each proper noun.

 Draft Book

Find a page of writing in your Draft Book. Underline the pronouns with red. Make corrections where necessary.

Name _____

 # Put Yourself Last ▶ order with I or me

When writing about yourself and other people, put yourself last in order.

example: Amy and I rode our bikes. (right)
I and Amy rode our bikes. (wrong)
She gave candy to Pete and me. (right)
She gave candy to me and Pete. (wrong)

Rewrite each sentence. Put the pronoun _I_ or _me_ where it belongs.

I and Max shot arrows at the target.

_____

Nellie showed the book to me and Chris.

_____

I and Horace played tag with Charlie.

_____

I and Amber closed the gate.

_____

Rico recited a poem to me and May.

_____

Victor sang "Drum Beat" with me and Oliver.

_____

I, Arla, and Tony shared the four scoops of ice cream.

_____

 ## Review Work

Underline the verb in
each sentence with blue.

 ## Draft Book

Write a story about yourself and a friend. Use the skill learned on this page.

Name _____

My Bike Bumped His Bike ▶ possessive pronouns

Possessive pronouns take the place of possessive nouns. They are: *my*, *your*, *his*, *her*, *its*, *our*, and *their*. The possessive pronoun *its* does not have an apostrophe.

Write the correct possessive pronoun on each line.

_____ chair bumped Arnie.
    Joanne's

Willa broke _____ glasses.
            Burt's

Rachel borrowed _____ markers.
                Meg's and my

We tossed _____ slimy bones.
          the dogs'

_____ ring is loud.
    The phone's

_____ car bumped our mailbox.
    My family's

Those blueberries stained _____ shirts.
                          Trevor's and Amy's

_____ computer downloaded that message.
    Cindy's

Write a sentence for each of the following pronouns: *my* and *your*.

_____

_____

🔍 **Review Work**

Underline the verb in each sentence with blue.

✏️ **Draft Book**

Write 10 sentences using possessive pronouns.

Name _____

▶ Mine, Ours, Theirs ▶ possessive pronouns

Possessive pronouns take the place of possessive nouns. They can be used before a noun or alone. The possessive pronoun *its* does not have an apostrophe.

before a noun: my, your, his, her, its, our, their
alone: mine, yours, his, hers, its, ours, theirs

Circle the correct pronoun.

Jan wants (my, mine) paper.

That plant is (her, hers).

(Our, Ours) house is the white one with blue trim.

Bring (your, yours) swimsuit along.

(Their, Theirs) car was parked next to the building.

Pete has (our, his) own paints, but he wants to borrow (her, hers).

Dad will buy me a swing set like (their, theirs).

That ice cream cone you ate was (my, mine).

We will bring (our, ours) lunches on the field trip.

(Her, Hers) scissors dropped on the floor.

That team lost their bat, so they borrowed (our, ours).

Kelly has a bike, but she wants to use (your, yours).

 Review Work

Write the verb tense beside each sentence: P = present, S = past, or F = future.

 Draft Book

Write 10 sentences using possessive pronouns. Use each possessive pronoun at least once.

Name _____

The simple subject of a sentence is the noun that the sentence is about.

example: Pat's **fish** swam in the aquarium.

example: Mount Everest is the tallest mountain in the world.

Circle the noun that is the subject of each sentence.

Mackinac Bridge spans the upper and lower peninsulas of Michigan.

Rick's shoelace needs to be tied.

The car needs gasoline.

The water is icy cold.

My cousin vacationed in Oregon.

Diamonds are compressed coal.

My dad mowed the lawn.

Marianas Trench is in the Pacific Ocean.

That list helps me remember things.

The baseball sailed over the fence.

Our sink is leaking and needs to be fixed.

Jorge plays tennis at Olsen Courts.

🔍 Review Work

Draw an X next to each proper noun that names a person. Draw a triangle above each proper noun that names a place.

✏️ Draft Book

Find a full page of writing in your Draft Book. Write an *SS* above the simple subject in each sentence.

▶ Subject Fill In

The simple subject of a sentence is the noun that the sentence is about.

example: Jon's **dog** is fluffy.

example: The **storm** blew the old building down.

Add a simple subject to each sentence, using a singular or plural noun as indicated. If a proper noun is used, capitalize it.

singular   A _____ helps people keep track of dates.

plural   _____ are fun to read.

singular   A _____ climbs trees.

plural   _____ soar through the sky.

plural   _____ go very fast.

plural   _____ are fruit.

singular   My _____ is tired.

singular   _____ likes to read.

singular   A _____ is delicious.

plural   _____ are far away.

plural   _____ drift in the water.

singular   _____ is an exciting game.

🔍 Review Work

Underline the nouns that are not simple subjects with yellow.

✏️ Draft Book

Find a full page of writing in your Draft Book. Write an *SS* above the simple subject in each sentence.

Name _____

▶ Keep It Simple

The simple predicate is the verb that tells what someone or something is doing.

example: Larry **kicked** the soccer ball for the winning goal.

Underline each simple predicate.

Fiona scrunched up her nose.

Marvin bounced on his bed.

Ellie rustled the bag of chips.

Mannie breezed through the entryway.

The swan paddled in the pond.

The dog tripped over my foot.

Alvin dated his paper.

Mrs. Tilley indented the paragraph.

The pudding splattered all over the floor.

Julie scurried to get her work done.

The dancers leaped across the stage.

Max created a new cookie.

Ollie ended his story.

 Review Work

Underline the nouns with yellow.

Draft Book

Use one sentence on this page in a story. Underline the simple predicates in your story with blue.

Name _____

► Entomology

The simple predicate is the verb that tells what someone or something is doing.

Underline each simple subject once. Underline the simple predicate twice.

Bees buzz.

A grasshopper hops.

Butterflies migrate.

A caterpillar crawls.

A dragonfly hovers.

A hornet stings.

Ants scurry.

Silkworms spin.

Ladybugs swarm.

A cicada hums.

Write the singular nouns with their verbs here.

_____   _____

_____   _____

_____

Write the plural nouns with their verbs here.

_____   _____

_____   _____

_____

 Review Work

Choose a sentence with a singular noun. Rewrite it to make the noun plural.

_____

 Draft Book

Find a page of writing in your Draft Book. Choose five sentences from that page and rewrite them. If a noun is singular, make it plural. If a noun is plural, make it singular. Remember to change each verb, too!

Name _____

▶ The Whole Thing ▷ complete subject

The simple subject is the noun that the sentence is about. The complete subject is the simple subject plus any articles or adjectives that describe or modify that noun.

example: The striped ball rolled down the hill.
ball = simple subject
The striped ball = complete subject

article   *adjective*

Circle the simple subject. Underline the complete subject.

My third-grade teacher wrote on the overhead projector.

The little, purple candy tingles on my tongue.

That enormous elephant trumpeted for an hour.

The glowing, hot lava poured down the hillside.

That skinny, black pen writes perfectly.

The noisy, bright, exciting carnival will close at 9:00.

Anna Rice will throw the ball.

Her new watch broke yesterday.

The large, fierce lion cowered in the corner.

The sticky glue spilled onto Brin's pants.

 Review Work

> Underline the simple predicates with blue. Write the verb tense beside each sentence: P = present, S = past, and F = future.

 Draft Book

> Write 10 sentences with articles or adjectives modifying the simple subjects. Circle the simple subjects and underline the complete subjects.

Name _____

Completeness ▶ complete subject

The simple subject is the noun that the sentence is about. The complete subject is the simple subject plus any articles or adjectives that describe or modify that noun.

example: The tall oak tree swayed in the breeze.
tree = simple subject
The tall oak tree = complete subject

article adjectives

Sometimes the simple subject is the complete subject.

example: Don ran home.

Don is the simple subject. Don is also the complete subject.

Circle the simple subject. Underline the complete subject.

Blaine weeded the garden.

Erika toured the village.

Winnie's little golden guinea pig ran under the dresser.

The overdone hamburgers tasted bad.

Horns blared on the street.

The recess bell rang.

Tim will make his bed.

An oxygen tank assists deep-sea divers.

Prickly cactus survive in hot deserts.

My ring fell into the sink.

🔍 Review Work

Underline the simple predicates with blue. Write the verb tense beside each sentence: P = present, S = past, and F = future.

✏️ Draft Book

Write 10 sentences with articles or adjectives modifying the simple subjects. Circle the simple subjects and underline the complete subjects.

▶ That One

complete subject

The complete subject is the simple subject plus any articles or adjectives that describe or modify that noun. It can also include other modifiers you have not yet learned to identify.

example: The (cup) of hot chocolate is empty.

The (monkey) by the feeding bowl threw a banana.

The (apple) with a bruise fell on the floor.

Circle the simple subject. Underline the complete subject.

That puppy by the bench dug this big hole.

The snorkeling group of 15 swam near the reef.

Flowers from that garden smell wonderful.

The canoe alongside the dock took me to the island.

The parrot with a green head will belong to Ned when he pays for it.

The brown horse brushed my shoulder with her nose.

The slimy earthworms in that pile of leaves are great fish bait.

The moldy bread in the garbage looks awful.

Frogs will swim in this pond when it's warmer.

That candle on the table burns brightly.

🔍 Review Work

Underline the simple predicates with blue. Write the verb tense beside each sentence: P = present, S = past, and F = future.

✏️ Draft Book

Write 10 sentences. Circle the simple subjects and underline the complete subjects.

► Here We Go

complete predicate

The simple predicate is the verb that tells what someone or something is doing. The complete predicate is the simple predicate plus any helping or linking verbs and any adverbs that describe or modify the verb.

example: The ball will roll smoothly.
roll = simple predicate
will roll smoothly = complete predicate

helping verb   *adverb*

Circle the simple predicate. Underline the complete predicate twice.

Jake often reads quickly.

The snow frequently fell rapidly.

The rain pounded loudly last night.

The wet dog shook vigorously.

An ant may have wandered around yesterday.

June never screams loudly.

That koala will eat constantly.

That lion could lunge immediately.

Lena may finish tonight.

Those tennis shoes smell awful.

 Review Work

Identify the verb tense of each sentence. Write the verb tense beside each sentence: P = present, S = past, and F = future.

 Draft Book

Write 10 sentences with helping or linking verbs and adverbs modifying the simple predicates. Circle the simple predicates and underline the complete predicates twice.

Name _____

▶ The Whole

The complete predicate is the simple predicate plus any helping or linking verbs, any adverbs, and any other words that tell where, when, why, or how the verb happens. If the words are not part of the complete subject, they are included in the complete predicate.

example: Bob will(bike) to the beach.

The big red apple (fell) to the ground.

Sally (played) with her brother.

Circle the simple predicate. Underline the complete predicate twice.

The glass of milk spilled onto Heidi's shoes.

Five tiny owlets hooted softly for a meal.

Chambers and Juanita guarded the soccer goals.

Miranda filled the bird feeder last week.

The raccoons destroyed the garden.

The hen will gobble up any feed it finds.

Zane wandered aimlessly through the toy store.

Nellie quickly subtracted a page of numbers.

Keith carefully sewed the button on his jacket.

Our family will attend the play next Tuesday.

A spider dangled above our heads.

 Review Work

Identify the verb tense of each sentence. Write the verb tense beside each sentence: P = present, S = past, and F = future.

 Draft Book

Write 10 sentences with helping or linking verbs and adverbs modifying the simple predicates. Circle the simple predicates and underline the complete predicates twice.

Name _____

▶ Do Tell

The complete subject tells who or what the sentence is about. The complete predicate tells what the someone or something is doing.

Underline the complete subject once. Underline the complete predicate twice.

The noisy movie prevented Kris from working.

The box of tissues emptied quickly.

The old, rusty swing continues to be the kids' favorite.

Pete loads the back of the truck with plants.

Many shiny marbles scattered across the tile floor.

Many important men signed the Declaration of Independence.

Few tomato plants survived the dog's digging.

The steep cliff towered above the river.

The remote-controlled car raced along the sidewalk.

The giant toad devoured many insects.

The tape secured the picture to the wall.

 Review Work

Write an *SS* above the simple subject in each sentence. Circle the simple predicates.

 Draft Book

Locate a page of writing in your Draft Book. Underline each complete subject once. Underline each complete predicate twice.

© Carson-Dellosa

Name _____

▶ Star or X   complete sentences

A sentence needs one complete subject and one complete predicate to be a sentence.

example: <u>Jan</u> <u>has a dog</u>. = sentence

　　　　　complete subject　complete predicate

　　　　　a dog = not a sentence

A sentence can be long or short.

example: <u>Jan</u> <u>walks</u>.

　　　　complete subject　complete predicate

example: <u>The tiny little bird with the broken wing</u> ← *complete subject*
<u>finally flew out the door and into the backyard</u>. ← *complete predicate*

If the group of words is a sentence, put a star in the box. Underline the complete subject once. Underline the complete predicate twice. If the group of words is not a sentence, put an X in the box.

☐ The old yellow lion in the cage.

☐ Walking through the quiet hallway.

☐ Many little.

☐ The strawberries are tasty.

☐ Are very large.

☐ In that really scary house.

☐ Camp is fun.

☐ Carrots are healthy.

☐ That butterfly is beautiful.

☐ Jake closed it.

☐ Josie walks to school.

☐ Going here?

☐ The woods are.

☐ This bubble gum.

🔍 Review Work

Write the linking verbs used in the groups of words from above.

_____

✏️ Draft Book

Make complete sentences using each group of words that has an X in the box.

Name _____

▶ Make the Fix   complete sentences

A sentence needs one complete subject and one complete predicate to be a sentence.

example: Jan has a dog. = sentence

complete subject   complete predicate

a dog = not a sentence

These groups of words are not sentences. Rewrite them as complete sentences. Put an uppercase letter at the beginning and correct punctuation at the end.

gallops towards

_____

should George

_____

gather those

_____

Leon's lizard

_____

ends at noon

_____

the enormous

_____

is incredible

_____

🔍 Review Work

Underline each complete subject once and each complete predicate twice.

✏️ Draft Book

Find a full page of writing in your Draft Book. Circle any groups of words that are not complete sentences and rewrite them so that they are complete.

► Is It Complete?

complete sentences

A group of words needs one complete subject and one complete predicate to be a sentence.

If the group of words is a sentence, put a star in the box. Underline the complete subject once and the complete predicate twice. If the group of words is not a sentence, put an X in the box.

The elephant is charging ☐

Reggie has three adorable kittens ☐

Jon colored the frog green ☐

That pair of scissors is sharp ☐

Did Sam collect the money ☐

Should this bike ☐

Can Rebecca go swimming ☐

Of red and blue paper ☐

Moaning and groaning ☐

The bluebird swooped down to grab an insect ☐

Will bats fly in the backyard tonight ☐

Dan's umbrella in the old bucket ☐

🔍 Review Work

Write a complete sentence with each phrase with an X in its box.

✏️ Draft Book

Find a full page of writing in your Draft Book. Circle any groups of words that are not complete sentences and rewrite them so that they are complete.

▶ Noun Modifiers ▶ prepositions

A preposition is a word that relates a noun to other words in the sentence. It can give more information as well as tell location (where a noun is), direction (where a noun is going), or time (when a noun happens). Some common prepositions are: *by, from, to, in, in front of, next to, of, under,* and *with.* The preposition must modify, or give more information about, the noun in the sentence, not the verb.

Circle the prepositions. Underline the nouns they are modifying.

Maddie would like a cup of hot chocolate.

The car next to the restaurant is ours.

Frida found her pencil under the couch.

The cookies in the jar are delicious.

The letter from my grandma came last night.

The seat in the middle is Jon's.

Kristi bought the goldfish with five black spots.

The bump in front of your sled will send you sailing.

The paper under the couch needs to be picked up.

The kittens with red collars are Mike's.

Stuart brought a bag of potato chips.

Bryan's skates are the ones with fluorescent orange wheels.

Lori is painting the window by the ladder.

Marshall wants a piece of pie.

 Review Work

Underline the verbs in the sentences with blue.

 Draft Book

Write a sentence for each preposition above.

► Tell Me Which One

prepositions

A preposition is a word that relates a noun to other words in the sentence. It can give more information as well as tell location (where a noun is), direction (where a noun is going), or time (when a noun happens). A preposition begins a phrase called a prepositional phrase.

noun modified

Meg drinks a cup(of)warm tea.

preposition   *prepositional phrase*

Prepositions include: *by, from, to, in, in front of, next to, of, under,* and *with.* The preposition must modify, or give more information about, the noun in the sentence, not the verb.

Circle the preposition. Underline the prepositional phrase. Draw an arrow to the noun it modifies.

The sweater with red stripes must be washed.

The student in the blue jacket is Kelwin.

Please get the pencil by the book.

The bats in the attic are sleeping.

The sandwich in that bag is moldy.

Madalen bought a doll with brown hair.

Krystal read a chapter from that book.

That desk next to mine is messy.

Check the atlas in the bookcase.

The bowl with cereal in it fell off the counter.

 Review Work
Underline the verbs in the sentences with blue.

 Draft Book
Write a sentence for each preposition above.

Name _____

▶ We Sound the Same ▶ homophones

Homophones are words that sound alike but are spelled differently and have different meanings.

Write the correct homophone on the line.

threw: verb, past tense of throw   **through:** between, from one side to another

Victoria walked _____ the door.

Paulina looked _____ the window.

Angelica _____ the winning pass.

sent: verb, past tense of send   **scent:** a smell   **cent:** unit of money

The _____ of that flower is faint.

Mr. Hill _____ Allison to the office.

This penny is worth one _____ .

its: possessive pronoun   **it's:** contraction for it is

_____ very hot outside.

The class has _____ own drinking fountain.

Brinley thinks _____ too cold to go in the pool.

_____ place is on that shelf.

whole: entire   **hole:** part missing

The _____ class is going on a field trip.

Jeremiah wanted the _____ apple.

There is a _____ in this sock.

🔍 Review Work

Underline the nouns with yellow.

✏️ Draft Book

Choose one pair of homophones. Write two sentences with each word.

We Sound the Same homophones

Homophones are words that sound alike but are spelled differently and have different meanings.

Write the correct homophone on the line.

no: antonym of yes   **know:** verb, to understand

_____ , you may not have any candy before dinner.

I don't _____ what street Julio lives on.

There are _____ dogs allowed here.

new: not old   **knew:** verb, past tense of know

Julian has a _____ bike.

Willow _____ where Paco lived.

The _____ theater has comfortable seats.

write: verb, to make purposeful marks, for example with a pencil
right: to be correct or a direction opposite of left

Put your name in the upper _____ corner.

Please _____ your name on the paper.

Yes, that answer is _____ .

allowed: permitted   **aloud:** out loud

We are not _____ to chew gum in school.

When you read _____ , it bothers me.

Are we _____ to bring pets to school?

Review Work

Underline the subject pronouns, object pronouns, and possessive pronouns with red.

Draft Book

Choose one pair of homophones. Write two sentences with each word.

Name _____

▶ We Sound the Same ▶ homophones

Homophones are words that sound alike but are spelled differently and have different meanings.

Write the correct homophone on the line.

here: location word   **hear:** to understand sound by way of the ear

Did you _____ the owl hooting last night?

They were _____ last night.

You can sit _____ beside me.

Sorry, I couldn't _____ you.

by: near   **buy:** to purchase

Put the pencil _____ the stack of books.

I would like to _____ that toy.

Where can I _____ new shoes?

Kelly is standing _____ the water fountain.

there: location word   **their:** possessive pronoun   **they're:** contraction for they are

Would you put this paper over _____ ?

He will go _____ for vacation.

Do you think _____ mother likes snakes?

_____ bringing a snake home.

I think _____ still in gym.

 Review Work

Underline the subject pronouns, object pronouns, and possessive pronouns with red.

Draft Book

Choose one pair of homophones. Write two sentences with each word.

Name _____

To, Too, Two   ▶ homophones

To, too, and two are homophones.

to is used in place of toward or with a verb: Rita went **to** school.
I like **to** eat candy.

two is a number word for the numeral 2: Ian has **two** sisters.

too means also or more than enough: Zane wants some milk, **too**.
That music is **too** noisy.

Write *to*, *too*, or *two* on each line.

talia left at _____ o'clock

is that soup _____ hot

are you tired, _____

_____ lions roared

my aunt plans _____ come _____ our soccer

game, _____

you can have _____ stickers, _____

toni went _____ _____ amusement parks this summer

anthony broke _____ crayons

we saw _____ hours of fireworks

angelica threw the ball _____ aaron

please give those _____ crickets _____ george

sheila will mail the letter _____ alicia

 Review Work

Add uppercase letters and ending punctuation.

Draft Book

Write three sentences with each meaning of these homophones.

▶ Evening

declarative sentences

A declarative sentence tells something. It begins with an uppercase letter and ends with a period.

Cross out the first letter of each sentence and write the uppercase letter next to it. Put a period at the end of each sentence.

the sky is beginning to darken ☐

a shooting star streaked across the sky ☐

i wonder how far away the nearest star is ☐

haley looked at stars through the telescope ☐

lourdes saw Jupiter and Venus last night ☐

the stars are not as bright as the moon ☐

many noises can be heard at night ☐

i don't like night noises that are scary ☐

the full moon is rising above the trees ☐

i heard an owl hoot ☐

it is time to go to bed ☐

🔍 Review Work

Circle the adjectives with orange.

✏️ Draft Book

Write six interrogative and six declarative sentences. Begin each sentence with an uppercase letter and end it with the correct punctuation mark.

Name _____

▶ I Want to Know ▷ interrogative sentences

An interrogative sentence asks a question. It begins with an uppercase letter and ends with a question mark.

Rewrite each interrogative sentence. Put an uppercase letter at the beginning and a question mark at the end.

who owns that red bike

_____

what kind of insect is that

_____

how did the kite get stuck in that tree

_____

where do fruit bats sleep

_____

who gave the Statue of Liberty to the United States

_____

do tarantulas live in Arkansas

_____

will you turn off that loud music

_____

are those cookies still hot

_____

 Review Work

Some of the sentences above have linking or helping verbs. Underline these verbs with blue.

 Draft Book

Write five interrogative sentences. Begin each sentence with an uppercase letter and end it with a question mark.

▶ Where?

declarative and interrogative sentences

A declarative sentence tells something and ends with a period. An interrogative sentence asks a question and ends with a question mark.

Put the correct punctuation mark at the end of each sentence. Answer the question with a declarative sentence using the information given.

Kangaroos live where koalas live ☐   Koalas live in Australia ☐

Where do kangaroos live ☐

_____

Wild penguins do not live north of the equator ☐ Alaska is north of the equator ☐

Do wild penguins live in Alaska ☐

_____

Monarch butterflies migrate to Michigan in the spring ☐   These butterflies migrate

to Mexico in the fall ☐   Are monarchs in Michigan in winter ☐

_____

Orangutans live in a small part of Southeast Asia ☐   The Brazilian rain forest is in

South America ☐   Do orangutans live in the Brazilian rain forest ☐

_____

🔍 Review Work

Choose one declarative sentence from each group of sentences. Underline the complete subject once. Underline the complete predicate twice.

✏️ Draft Book

Write your own set of interrogative and declarative sentences. Begin each sentence with an uppercase letter and end it with the correct punctuation mark.

Name _____

 **Wow!** **exclamatory sentences**

An exclamatory sentence shows strong feelings and ends with an exclamation mark.

Rewrite each exclamatory sentence. Put uppercase letters where they belong and exclamation marks at the ends.

this dessert is delicious

_____

that comet is breathtaking

_____

we're going to florida

_____

ouch, get off my foot

_____

you startled me

_____

the fireworks are incredible

_____

i did not crack that plate

_____

 Review Work

Choose one sentence from above and draw a star next to it. Pretend that sentence is the answer and write a question for it.

_____

Draft Book

Write five exclamatory sentences. Begin each sentence with an uppercase letter and end it with an exclamation mark.

Name _____

▶ Amusement Park
declarative, interrogative, and exclamatory sentences

A declarative sentence tells something and ends with a period. An interrogative sentence asks a question and ends with a question mark. An exclamatory sentence shows strong feelings and ends with an exclamation mark.

Put the correct punctuation mark at the end of each sentence. Write *declarative, interrogative,* **or** *exclamatory* **on the line.**

our class is going to the amusement park ☐ _____

the bus will leave early ☐ _____

did you set your alarm clock ☐ _____

abby and i stood in line together ☐ _____

yikes, the food here is expensive ☐ _____

did you bring lunch ☐ _____

i'm glad i did ☐ _____

we put our lunches into lockers ☐ _____

let's go to the rides ☐ _____

mona, julie, max, and i get in line for a roller coaster ☐ _____

we put on our seat belts and harnesses ☐ _____

i'm scared ☐ _____

🔍 Review Work

Review the sentence for words that should start with uppercase letters. Cross out the lowercase letters and write the uppercase letters above them.

✏️ Draft Book

Write three declarative, three interrogative, and three exclamatory sentences. Begin each sentence with an uppercase letter and end it with the correct punctuation mark.

Name _____

▶ Now Do This

imperative sentences

A sentence that tells you what to do or gives you a command is called an imperative sentence. An imperative sentence usually ends with a period.

Rewrite these imperative sentences. Put an uppercase letter at the beginning of each sentence and a period at the end.

buckle your seat belt

_____

obey traffic signals

_____

put on your helmet before riding your bike

_____

start all sentences with uppercase letters

_____

turn off those lights

_____

always capitalize proper nouns

_____

finish your work

_____

put a period at the end of a declarative sentence

_____

 Review Work

Underline the verbs in the sentences with blue.

 Draft Book

Write five imperative sentences. Begin each sentence with an uppercase letter and end it with a period.

Name _____

▶ With Feeling ⟩ imperative sentences

A sentence that tells you what to do or gives you a command is called an imperative sentence. Most imperative sentences end with periods. Occasionally, a command is given with great feeling. In this case, an exclamation mark is used. The same command can end with either a period or an exclamation mark depending on the situation.

example: Sit down. → Mom is asking you to sit down to dinner.
                Sit down! → A small child is standing on a rocking chair, and it is about to tip over.

Read the situation. Put the correct punctuation at the end of each imperative sentence.

Don't touch that ☐   The burner was just turned off and is still extremely hot.

Don't touch that ☐   Dad put a bowl of carrots on the table for dinner.

Hold still ☐   Five hornets are flying around.

Hold still ☐   Kyle is tying his brother's shoe.

Come here ☐   Your dog tries to wander into the woods at night.

Come here ☐   Willie wants to tell Hilda something.

Shut the gate ☐   Nan left the gate open.

Shut the gate ☐   The neighbor's dog is coming.

Stop that ☐   Ann tapped her brother on the shoulder.

Stop that ☐   Ann's little brother is trying to light matches.

🔍 Review Work
Underline the verbs in the sentences with blue.

✏️ Draft Book
Write eight imperative sentences. Begin each sentence with an uppercase letter. End some of the sentences with periods and some with exclamation marks. Describe each situation where you use an exclamation mark.

         © Carson-Dellosa

Name _____

▶ You, That's Who ▶ subject of imperative sentences

A sentence that tells you what to do or gives you a command is called an imperative sentence. An imperative sentence usually ends with a period. An imperative sentence looks like a complete predicate. The complete subject is *you*. *You* is implied, which means that since the speaker is talking to you, it is understood that *you* is the subject even though the word *you* isn't written.

Underline the complete predicate twice. Circle the simple predicate. Remember that in each sentence, the subject is *you*.

Run to the mailbox and get the mail.

Always capitalize the word "I."

Put the blanket over the birdcage.

Swat the mosquito above your head.

Get into bed immediately.

Don't spill juice on the carpet.

Brush your teeth every morning and night.

Write Grandma a thank-you note tonight.

Hold the ladder while I wash the window.

Stick the stamp on the corner of the envelope.

Please work quietly.

Ride slowly down that steep hill.

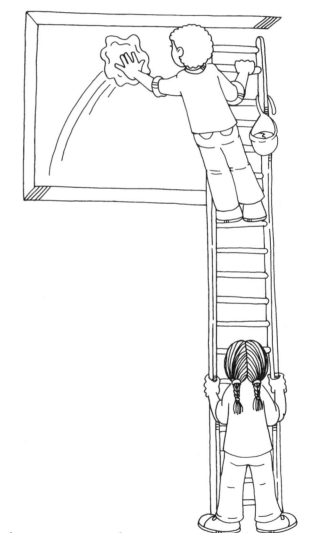

 Review Work

Circle the adverbs with purple.

 Draft Book

Write 10 imperative sentences. Begin each sentence with an uppercase letter and end it with a period.

Hiding Adjectives

predicate adjectives

Adjectives describe nouns. Predicates refer to verbs. A predicate adjective is an adjective that follows a linking verb. It is part of the complete predicate but it describes the simple subject.

example: The monster was <u>gigantic</u>.

Circle the predicate adjectives. Draw an arrow from each adjective to the noun it describes.

This cave is scary.

Silvia is helpful.

That huge tractor is muddy.

The three children were tired.

Ann was angry.

The dough is squishy.

The trailer was empty.

The class has been quiet.

That towering cliff is beautiful!

That assignment was difficult.

The new tape is sticky.

 ## Review Work

Underline each complete subject once and each complete predicate twice.

 ## Draft Book

Write 10 sentences that use predicate adjectives. Underline each predicate adjective and draw an arrow to the noun it describes. Underline the linking verbs with blue. Begin each sentence with an uppercase letter.

Name _____

▶ It Was Done to Whom? ▶ direct objects

A direct object is the noun that receives the action of the verb. It is located in the complete predicate. To locate the direct object, find the verb. Find a noun after the verb. If the verb is acting on the noun, the noun is the direct object.

example: The ball hit Emily.

verb   *noun*

Emily is the direct object because the ball hit or acted on her.

example: I sent David some money.

verb   *nouns*

Money is the direct object because the money was sent, not David.

Circle the verb. Draw an arrow to the direct object it affects.

The crab snapped his claws at the fish.

The starfish ate the clam.

The window air conditioner cooled the room.

The whale's tail smacked the water.

Five red ants carried off that beetle.

Jenna threw the markers across the table.

The dolphin can locate food with sonar.

Over time, coral builds islands.

The floating jellyfish stung the swimmer.

Wally rode his bike down the road.

Review Work

Underline the complete subject of each sentence.

Draft Book

Write four sentences using direct objects. Underline the direct object in each sentence with green.

▶ Just a Piece

phrases and clauses

A phrase is a group of words that does not have a subject and predicate. A clause is a group of words with a subject and a predicate. An independent clause can stand alone as a sentence. A dependent clause cannot stand alone as a sentence.

Write *P* if the group of words is a phrase. Write *IC* if the group of words is an independent clause. Add uppercase letters and punctuation, if needed. Write *DC* if the group of words is a dependent clause.

_____ Umberto has the flu

_____ whenever you can

_____ the enormous cookie

_____ the snake coiled around the stick

_____ back and forth

_____ because Jeffrey is helpful

_____ Nora will baby-sit them tonight

_____ orange, red, and yellow

_____ in the large jar

_____ after the rain stops

_____ by the bushes

_____ sticking to the wall

_____ soft, velvety fur

 Review Work

Underline the nouns with yellow and the verbs with blue.

 Draft Book

Use the phrases and dependent clauses to write complete sentences.

Name _____

▶ Combining Sentences ⟩ coordinating conjunctions

Sentences can be combined when their ideas are the same. Related sentences can be joined with coordinating conjunctions. There are seven coordinating conjunctions: *and, nor, but, for, yet, so,* and *or.*

examples: Kim eats her sandwich. + Kim eats her grapes. =
Kim eats her sandwich and her grapes.
Kim eats her sandwich. + Kim did not eat her grapes. =
Kim eats her sandwich but not her grapes.

Combine these sets of sentences. Write the new sentences on the lines.

Anika slept on the plane. Anika did not sleep on the train.

_____

Meg played with Maddie. Meg played with Jade.

_____

The pencil isn't new. The eraser isn't new.

_____

Aidan plays tennis. Aidan plays basketball.

_____

Stefano likes strawberries. Stefano does not like blueberries.

_____

The bat pup is soft. The bat pup is fuzzy.

_____

Pepe finished his math. Pepe did not finish his reading.

_____

 Review Work

Underline the complete subjects once and the complete predicates twice.

 Draft Book

Write three pairs of sentences that can be combined. Write a combined sentence for each pair.

Name _____

▶ Put Them Together

combining sentences

Sentences can be combined when their ideas are the same. Related sentences can be joined with coordinating conjunctions. There are seven coordinating conjunctions: *and, nor, but, for, yet, so,* and *or.*

Subjects can be combined to create a compound subject.

> **example:** Meg jumped on the trampoline. + Val jumped on the trampoline. = Meg and Val jumped on the trampoline.
>
> Meg jumped on the trampoline. + Val did not jump on the trampoline. = Meg but not Val jumped on the trampoline.

Use conjunctions to combine these sentences. Write the new sentences on the lines.

Ants live in communities. Bees live in communities.

_____

Penguins live in Antarctica. Polar bears do not live in Antarctica.

_____

Alison climbed the stairs. Eve climbed the stairs.

_____

Paul read that book. Mary did not read that book.

_____

The little gray duck swam in the pond. The baby swan swam in the pond.

_____

Starfish live in the ocean. Anemones live in the ocean.

_____

 Review Work

Underline the complete subjects once and the complete predicates twice.

 Draft Book

Write five sets of sentences whose subjects can be combined. Trade with a partner and combine the sentences.

Name _____

Doing Many Things

Sentences can be combined when their ideas are the same. Related sentences can be joined with coordinating conjunctions. There are seven coordinating conjunctions: *and*, *nor*, *but*, *for*, *yet*, *so*, and *or*.

Verbs can be combined to create a compound predicate.

    example: Jon planted the seeds. + Jon watered the seeds. =
                   Jon planted and watered the seeds.

Use conjunctions to combine these sentences. Write the new sentences on the lines.

Hal weeded the garden. Hal watered the garden.

_____

The bird caught insects. The bird ate insects.

_____

Renee slipped on the ice. Renee fell on the ice.

_____

The snake slid through the grass. The snake slithered through the grass.

_____

The chocolate was warmed. The chocolate was melted.

_____

Nola hangs the picture. Nola straightens the picture.

_____

Ian filled the water balloon. Ian threw the water balloon.

_____

 Review Work

    Underline the nouns with yellow and the verbs with blue.

 Draft Book

    Write five pairs of sentences whose predicates can be combined. Write a combined sentence for each pair.

And, And, And ▶ combining sentences

Sentences can be combined when their ideas are the same. Related sentences can be joined with coordinating conjunctions. There are seven coordinating conjunctions: *and, nor, but, for, yet, so,* and *or.*

Circle the coordinating conjunctions. If the sentence has a compound subject, write *CS*. If the sentence has a compound predicate, write *CP*. If it has both, write *B.*

_____ Joey and Olivia walk in the parade.

_____ Gwen grabbed and climbed the rope.

_____ The monkey hit the window and pounded on the wall.

_____ The thief grabbed her purse and ran for the door.

_____ The carpet and the couch need cleaning.

_____ The ants and beetles scurried and hid.

_____ Mia grabs the door and slams it.

_____ Candies and peanuts fell on the floor and rolled around.

_____ Your bedroom and the living room are messy.

_____ Melea and Rhonda swim and dive in the lake.

🔍 Review Work

Underline the simple subjects with yellow and simple predicates with blue.

✏️ Draft Book

Write five sentences with compound subjects, compound predicates, or both.

Name _____

▶ Check the Verb ⟩ combining sentences, subject-verb agreement

Sentences can be combined when their ideas are the same. Sometimes the verb must be changed when the subject changes from singular to plural.

example: Jan <u>likes</u> milk. + Tom <u>likes</u> milk. = Jan and Tom <u>like</u> milk.

Put a box around each conjunction. Circle the correct verb.

The teddy bear and the doll (sit, sits) on her pillow.

Rita and Erlina (slide, slides) down the twisty slide.

The lion and tiger (is, are) pacing in their cages.

The gray car and the white van (was, were) washed today.

That large horsefly and this buzzing mosquito (fly, flies) through the open door.

The large snail and that orange and black goldfish (live, lives) in this aquarium.

The hot tub and the pool (is, are) empty.

Roland and Gerald (enjoy, enjoys) music with a fast beat.

Juicy hot dogs and puffy, white marshmallows (toast, toasts) over the campfire.

My blue pajamas and fuzzy slippers (is, are) packed.

 Review Work

Underline the nouns with yellow. Draw an arrow from each adjective to the noun it describes.

 Draft Book

Write five sets of sentences whose subjects can be combined. Trade with a partner and combine the sentences. Watch subject-verb agreement!

Name _____

 **No Run-Ons** > independent clauses and conjunctions

When two independent clauses are written together, they create a run-on sentence. Two related independent clauses can be joined into one sentence with a coordinating conjunction. There are seven coordinating conjunctions: *and, nor, but, for, yet, so,* and *or.* A comma and a conjunction are needed to join two independent clauses into one sentence to avoid a run-on.

example: Jasmin needs a nap, <u>or</u> she may fall asleep.

subject predicate conjunction subject predicate

Circle each comma and coordinating conjunction.

Todd likes art, but he likes math better.

Emmie baked a batch of cookies, yet nobody wanted to eat one.

Misty needs to finish her paper now, or she will have to finish at recess.

Lola raced to the post office, but it was already closed.

Mom hemmed my pants, so I won't step on the bottoms.

Dana's pencil broke, so she sharpened it.

The puppy begged for a treat, but no one gave him one.

Theresa fell asleep at five o'clock, and she slept through the night.

Alvin played with me at recess, and he promised to eat lunch with me.

Wendell missed the winning basket, so he will practice every night this week.

 Review Work

Write an *SS* above each simple subject. Underline each simple predicate with blue.

 Draft Book

Write five sentences that join independent clauses with commas and conjunctions.

Name _____

 # Two or One?

When two independent clauses are written together, they create a run-on sentence. To correct a run-on, decide where the first sentence ends and the second begins. The clauses can remain in one sentence if they are separated by a comma and a coordinating conjunction. There are seven coordinating conjunctions: *and, nor, but, for, yet, so,* and *or.*

example: The stars were coming out the moon wasn't up yet. =
The stars were coming out, but the moon wasn't up yet.

Separate each run-on sentence with a comma and a conjunction. Rewrite each sentence correctly on the line. Circle each comma and coordinating conjunction.

Jade caught a starfish she didn't keep it.

_____

The sun was bright it burned my shoulders.

_____

Zoe answered every question they were all wrong.

_____

Hope had two sandwiches she gave one to Rob.

_____

The snow was great for packing Jill made a snowman.

_____

Our class was studying sedimentary rocks Ali brought in a fossil.

_____

 Review Work

Underline the nouns with yellow and the verbs with blue.

 Draft Book

Write five sentences that join independent clauses with commas and conjunctions.

Name _____

▶ Breaking

run-on sentences

When two independent clauses are written together, they create a run-on sentence. To avoid a run-on, decide where the first sentence ends and the second begins. A run-on can be corrected by separating it into two sentences by adding punctuation and an uppercase letter.

example: The lion is huge he looks fierce. = The lion is huge. He looks fierce.

Separate the run-on sentences. Rewrite them correctly on the lines.

Jeff has a brother his name is Rob.

_____

The clouds were dark they looked like rain clouds.

_____

That bench is wet it was just painted.

_____

Belle's nose is runny she has a cold.

_____

Alfred would like a dog he wants one with shaggy hair.

_____

I love eating watermelon they are so juicy.

_____

 Review Work

Choose two of the run-on sentences above and rewrite them. Join the independent clauses with commas and conjunctions.

 Draft Book

Look through the writing in your Draft Book for run-on sentences and correct them.

© Carson-Dellosa

Name _____

▶ Stop and Start ▶ run-on sentences

When two independent clauses are written together, they create a run-on sentence. To avoid a run-on, decide where the first sentence ends and the second begins. A run-on can be corrected by separating it into two sentences by adding punctuation and an uppercase letter.

example: Casey is helpful he sets the table every night. =
Casey is helpful. He sets the table every night.

Separate the run-on sentences. Put a punctuation mark at the end of the first sentence. Cross out the lowercase letter and write an uppercase letter above it to begin the second sentence.

Raven has a new backpack it is green with many zippers.

Ray needs a paper clip he needs it to hold his papers.

Katie borrowed my pencil she plans to make a map.

It is so cold the driveway is full of ice.

Jane is outside she is on the swings.

Zach is helping Dad Elroy is helping Dad, too.

Keesha read that book she recommended it to the class.

Tori found a baby squirrel it was lying at the bottom of that tree.

Zeke loves cinnamon rolls the ones with the nuts are his favorite.

Turn off the light it has been on too long.

 Review Work

Underline the complete subjects once and the complete predicates twice.

 Draft Book

Write 10 run-on sentences. Trade with a partner and correct the run-on sentences by separating them into complete sentences.

Name _____

What Do We Have Here?

Commas are used to group three or more common words.

nouns = Abby, Jena, and Zack went skiing.
verbs = Max can race, hurdle, and jump.
adjectives = This muddy, red, cotton shirt should be washed in cold water.
adverbs = The bee flew over, under, and around our desks.

Circle each comma. Write whether it is separating nouns, verbs, adjectives, or adverbs.

Jeff slowly, quietly, and carefully tiptoes past the sleeping baby.   _____

Melanie drew a picture of the large, bright, sunny yard.   _____

The golf ball bounced, rolled, and dropped into the cup.   _____

Tanya gulped the glass of fresh, icy, sour lemonade.   _____

Bruce saw emeralds, garnets, and rubies in the glass case.   _____

Leah rolled, folded, and taped the paper around the present.   _____

I love fresh, warm, crisp, chocolate chip cookies.   _____

Fred, Benny, Willow, and Bria watched the movie.   _____

Sign your name clearly, carefully, yet quickly.   _____

They played, swam, and ate at the beach.   _____

Willie was cranky, tired, and hungry.   _____

Sam peeled, dipped, and ate the shrimp.   _____

Review Work

Find the sentence with predicate adjectives. Draw a star next to it.

Draft Book

Write 10 sentences each with a list of three or more words. Put commas between the words in the lists.

© Carson-Dellosa

Name _____

▶ Tell Me How Many

Commas are used to group three or more common words or word groups.

Circle each comma. Answer the question.

Neil, Sandra, Rocky, Bruce, Olive, Gabriella, Jenna, and I were in the same group on the field trip.

How many people were in the group? _____

Kira needs to wash her face, brush her teeth, comb her hair, and change her socks before we leave.

How many things does Kira need to do? _____

We have green beans, baby carrots, potatoes, lettuce, spinach, and cucumbers in the refrigerator.

How many types of vegetables are in the refrigerator? _____

Our ice cream choices are vanilla, chocolate, strawberry, caramel nut, or cheesecake.

How many flavor choices are there? _____

Include three other things that could be found in the woods. Add commas where needed.

Paloma found an acorn _____ _____ and _____ on her walk through the woods.

🔍 Review Work

Underline the nouns with yellow and the verbs with blue.

✏️ Draft Book

Chose one of the above sentences and illustrate it.

Name _____

▶ Commas in Dates

A comma is a type of punctuation mark used to separate a group of three or more words in a list or series. Commas are also used in certain dates to separate the day of the week, the month and date, and the year.

yes: Tuesday, July 15
yes: Tuesday, July 15, 2003
yes: July 15, 2003
no: July 15
no: July 2003

Add commas and uppercase letters where needed in the dates.

monday august 19 1991

november 4 2000

wednesday march 26

december 1999

sunday september 12

friday january 17

april 1

thursday july 31 2003

february 1962

october 26 1998

Trish was born sunday january 6 2002.

Britt's birthday is june 29.

Ben started kindergarten tuesday august 27 2002.

Bailey will graduate in june 2012.

The program is thursday february 15.

 Review Work

Choose two complete dates that include the day of the week, month, date, and year. Rewrite them using abbreviations.

_____

_____

Draft Book

Write 10 sentences using dates. Add commas where needed.

▶ Now Read This ▶ quotation marks

Some titles need quotation marks around them.

article titles from magazines and newspapers: I read "Drums Are Beating" in the Wednesday paper.

chapter titles in a book: The chapter "Moon Phases" was interesting.

song and poem titles: We sang "Row, Row, Row Your Boat" in music today.

Book titles, however, do not need quotation marks. Book titles are underlined.

Add quotation marks where they belong. Underline book titles.

The chapter Summertime in the book A Year with Me talked about gardening.

I will read No Bikes Allowed when you hand me the newspaper.

The headline on this page says Meteor Shower Tonight.

Iris played Marching Along on her flute.

Zane's favorite song is Tennis Shoe Run.

Did you read Evermore Evening? I'm on the fifth chapter called Stars Come Out.

You should read this article called How to Be Nice to Your Little Sister.

Ernie's birds like to sing when Birdie Bop plays on the radio.

I think the poem Bellybutton is funny.

Kale's favorite book is Up and Down.

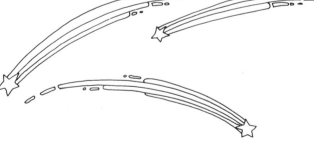

🔍 Review Work

Underline the simple predicates with blue.

✏️ Draft Book

Write eight sentences using titles. Use the skill learned on this page to punctuate titles.

▶ My Turn

▶ quotation marks

Direct quotations are treated in a special way. The first word of a direct quotation is capitalized. Quotation marks go around the words people say. Punctuation at the end or at a break in the direct quote goes inside the quotation marks.

example: "You did a great job!" said Tom. "This is fun," said Rob.

Add quotation marks around the words people say. Circle all uppercase letters and punctuation inside quotation marks.

Knock it off, growled Andy.

Make me! yelled Tara.

Hey, wait a minute, interrupted Jon. That's no way to solve a problem.

You're right, agreed Andy. Listen, Tara, I wanted you to stop jumping in front of me. I'm trying to make a basket.

Yeah, but I've asked you bunches of times if I could have a turn, and you've ignored me, retorted Tara.

You did? questioned Andy.

Yes, I did, answered Tara. That's the only class ball, and you told me this morning we could share it.

I did, didn't I, gulped Andy, But you still didn't have to get mad. You could have just talked to me then.

I guess, said Tara. I was just so frustrated that I yelled. I shouldn't have. Sorry.

Apology accepted, said Andy. I'm sorry I ignored you. I'll have to concentrate on listening better.

Thanks, accepted Tara. So, how about giving me a turn?

Review Work

Underline the verbs used in place of *said* with blue.

Draft Book

Write a story that contains direct quotations. Use the skills learned from this page to add quotation marks and punctuation.

Name _____

▶ Dear Friend

Letters have five parts: date, greeting, body, closing, and signature. The words in greetings and closings begin with uppercase letters. They end with commas. The greeting, closing, and signature have their own lines.

January 2, 2002   ← date

Dear Grandpa,   ← greeting

    Thank you for taking me fishing. I liked catching all of those fish. They tasted great for dinner. I hope we ← body catch more when we go again.

      Love,   ← closing

      Tricia   ← signature

Fill in the missing parts to these letters. Label each part.

_____   ← _____

Dear _____ ,   ← _____

    You are invited to my house for a sleepover. Please let me know if you can come.   ← body

      Sincerely,   ← closing

      Chelsea Brent   ← signature

_____   ← _____

_____   ← _____

    I went to the library on Monday. I chose five books and listened to a great storyteller. I hope you ← body can meet me there next Monday.

_____   ← _____

_____   ← _____

🔍 Review Work

Circle all uppercase letters and punctuation marks.

✏️ Draft Book

Write a letter to a friend. Include all of the parts listed above.

▶ Not Correct

The sentences below have many mistakes. Rewrite the sentences and make the corrections.

the box of apples are in the trunk of jerries car

_____

yous is mean said allie you never share with me and jane

_____

tom sat lays and digging in the dirt at tunnel park

_____

mine cup of nuts are on the counter dont eat it

_____

i and jason went to st louis missouri on monday october 14

_____

_____

why is they're to candy bars instead of five

_____

i pete and joe is hear we wants too watching the movie

_____

_____

▶ Identify the Parts ▷ review

Tell as much about each sentence as you can. What kind of sentence is it? What tense is it written in? Underline nouns with yellow and verbs with blue. Draw boxes around adjectives. Circle adverbs with purple.

Meg and Maddie will kick the ball.

    kind: ☐ declarative ☐ interrogative ☐ exclamatory ☐ imperative

    tense: ☐ past ☐ present ☐ future

The shoes with red laces were lost.

    kind: ☐ declarative ☐ interrogative ☐ exclamatory ☐ imperative

    tense: ☐ past ☐ present ☐ future

Did a little redbird quickly fly past?

    kind: ☐ declarative ☐ interrogative ☐ exclamatory ☐ imperative

    tense: ☐ past ☐ present ☐ future

This ice cream is delicious!

    kind: ☐ declarative ☐ interrogative ☐ exclamatory ☐ imperative

    tense: ☐ past ☐ present ☐ future

Name _____

▶ Student Editing Checklist

Check each highlighted item*

☐ Each sentence contains a complete subject and a complete predicate.

☐ Each sentence can be identified as one of the following:

    ☐ Declarative   ☐ Interrogative   ☐ Exclamatory   ☐ Imperative

☐ Sentences that can be combined have been combined.

☐ There are no run-on sentences.

☐ The first letter in each sentence is capitalized, including the first letter inside quotation marks.

☐ The pronoun I is always capitalized.

☐ Each word that names a day, month, or holiday starts with an uppercase letter.

☐ Each proper noun starts with an uppercase letter.

☐ Each title starts with an uppercase letter.

☐ Each declarative or imperative sentence ends with a period.

☐ Each interrogative sentence ends with a question mark.

☐ Each exclamatory sentence ends with an exclamation mark.

☐ Commas are used to separate dates.

☐ Commas are used in the greeting and closing in a letter.

☐ Commas are used in a list or series of three or more words.

☐ A comma is used between a city and state.

☐ Two independent clauses are joined with a conjunction and a comma.

☐ Abbreviations end with periods.

☐ Quotation marks are used around direct quotations, and certain titles.

☐ Book titles are underlined.

* Teacher highlights items for individual student edit.

Name _____

▶ Student Editing Checklist (cont.)

☐ A plural noun usually ends in *s* or *es*.

☐ A possessive noun usually ends in *'s*.

☐ Subject pronouns come before verbs.

☐ Object pronouns come after verbs.

☐ Possessive pronouns take the place of possessive nouns.

☐ All verb tenses correctly describe when something is happening.

☐ Singular verbs follow singular nouns.

☐ Plural verbs follow plural nouns.

☐ Prefixes are placed at the beginnings of words.

☐ Suffixes are placed at the ends of words.

☐ Words are spelled correctly for their meanings.

☐ Articles are used before nouns or adjective/noun combinations.

☐ Apostrophes take the place of dropped letters in contractions.

☐ Other:

_____

_____

_____

Page 6

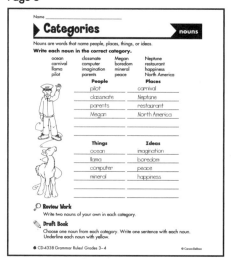

Categories — nouns

Nouns are words that name people, places, things, or ideas.
Write each noun in the correct category.

ocean, carnival, llama, pilot, classmate, computer, imagination, parents, Megan, boredom, mineral, peace, Neptune, restaurant, happiness, North America

People	Places
pilot	carnival
classmate	Neptune
parents	restaurant
Megan	North America

Things	Ideas
ocean	imagination
llama	boredom
computer	peace
mineral	happiness

Review Work
Write two nouns of your own in each category.

Draft Book
Choose one noun from each category. Write one sentence with each noun. Underline each noun with yellow.

6 CD-4338 Grammar Rules! Grades 3–4 © Carson-Dellosa

RW: Answers will vary. DB: Answers will vary.

Page 7

Find the Nouns — nouns

Nouns are words that name people, places, things, or ideas.
Underline the nouns in the sentences.

Ellie has a wonderful idea.
Tarantulas live in Arizona.
Max went to the course to play golf with his brother.
That turtle in the sink belongs to Anna.
The computer printed six pages of text.
Simon always encouraged Gwen's creativity.
Ian fertilized the plants by the window.
The boots in the hallway belong to Pam.

Review Work
Write the nouns from the sentences in the correct categories.

People:	Ellie	brother	Simon	Ian
	Max	Anna	Gwen	Pam
Places:	course	Arizona		
	hallway			
Things:	tarantulas	turtle	computer	text	window
	golf	sink	pages	plants	boots
Ideas:	idea			
	creativity			

Draft Book
Make lists of people you know, places you have been, and things that interest you. These are all nouns! Include at least 10 nouns in each list. Use these nouns in future writing assignments.

CD-4338 Grammar Rules! Grades 3–4 7

DB: Answers will vary.

Page 8

Names — common and proper nouns

Common nouns are nouns that name unspecific or general people, places, things, or ideas. Proper nouns are nouns that name specific people, places, things, or ideas. A proper noun always starts with an uppercase letter. A person's first and last names are proper nouns. Titles like Mr., Mrs., Miss, Ms., and Dr. are proper nouns, too.
examples: girl, president, leader (common nouns)
examples: Sarah Berg, President Lincoln, Martin Luther King, Jr. (proper nouns)
Write each noun in the correct category. Capitalize the proper nouns.

cory, doctor, teammate, carol hobin, lynette, artist, judge, golden gate bridge, mr. prince, dr. desmond, student, sam smith, parent, florida, cook, editor

Common Nouns	Proper Nouns
teammate	Florida
judge	Lynette
doctor	Carol Hobin
artist	Golden Gate Bridge
student	Mr. Prince
parent	Dr. Desmond
cook	Sam Smith
editor	Cory

Review Work
Write two nouns of your own in each category.

Draft Book
Write five sentences. Use a proper noun that names a person in each sentence.

8 CD-4338 Grammar Rules! Grades 3–4 © Carson-Dellosa

RW: Answers will vary. DB: Answers will vary.

Page 9

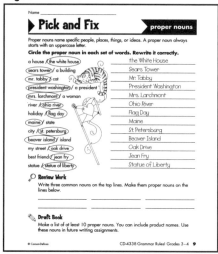

Pick and Fix — proper nouns

Proper nouns name specific people, places, things, or ideas. A proper noun always starts with an uppercase letter.
Circle the proper noun in each set of words. Rewrite it correctly.

a house / the white house → the White House
sears tower / a building → Sears Tower
mr. tabby / cat → Mr. Tabby
president washington / a president → President Washington
mrs. larchmont / a woman → Mrs. Larchmont
river / ohio river → Ohio River
holiday / flag day → Flag Day
maine / state → Maine
city / st. petersburg → St. Petersburg
beaver island / island → Beaver Island
my street / oak drive → Oak Drive
best friend / jean fry → Jean Fry
statue / statue of liberty → Statue of Liberty

Review Work
Write three common nouns on the top lines. Make them proper nouns on the lines below.

Draft Book
Make a list of at least 10 proper nouns. You can include product names. Use these nouns in future writing assignments.

CD-4338 Grammar Rules! Grades 3–4 9

RW: Answers will vary. DB: Answers will vary.

Page 10

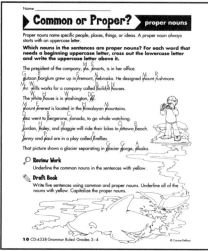

Common or Proper? — proper nouns

Proper nouns name specific people, places, things, or ideas. A proper noun always starts with an uppercase letter.
Which nouns in the sentences are proper nouns? For each word that needs a beginning uppercase letter, cross out the lowercase letter and write the uppercase letter above it.

The president of the company, ms. smarts, is in her office.
gutzon borglum grew up in fremont, nebraska. He designed mount rushmore.
mr. wills works for a company called buildit houses.
The white house is in washington, dc.
mount everest is located in the himalayan mountains.
zez went to bergerone, canada, to go whale watching.
jordan, haley, and maggie will ride their bikes to ottawa beach.
jenny and paul are in a play called fireflies.
That picture shows a glacier separating in glacier gorge, alaska.

Review Work
Underline the common nouns in the sentences with yellow.

Draft Book
Write five sentences using common and proper nouns. Underline all of the nouns with yellow. Capitalize the proper nouns.

10 CD-4338 Grammar Rules! Grades 3–4 © Carson-Dellosa

RW: Underline president, company, office, company, whale watching, bikes, play, picture, and glacier with yellow.
DB: Answers will vary.

Page 11

Here and There — proper nouns

Proper nouns name specific people, places, things, or ideas. A proper noun always starts with an uppercase letter. When proper nouns name a city and state, a comma goes between them.
example: Orlando, Florida

Write the names and addresses correctly. Capitalize the proper nouns. Put commas between the city and state names.

mr. m. t. headler → Mr. M. T. Headler
9210 polk boulevard → 9210 Polk Boulevard
littletown ohio 45678 → Littletown, Ohio 45678

mrs. s. o. socking → Mrs. S.O. Socking
86 dampness drive → 86 Dampness Drive
verywet washington 98110 → Verywet, Washington 98110

For each proper noun that needs a beginning uppercase letter, cross out the lowercase letter and write the uppercase letter above it. Put commas between the city and state names.

olga and ron's family plans to take a trip to portland, oregon.
andrew's grandmother lives in sheboygan, wisconsin.
walter stopped in pierre, south dakota, on his way to mount rushmore.

Review Work
In the sentences, draw an X next to each proper noun that names a person. Draw a triangle above each proper noun that names a place.

Draft Book
Write your name and address. Capitalize all of the proper nouns. Put a comma between the names of your city and state.

© Carson-Dellosa CD-4338 Grammar Rules! Grades 3–4 11

RW: Draw an X next to Olga, Ron, Andrew, and Walter. Draw a triangle above Portland, Oregon, Sheboygan, Wisconsin, Pierre, South Dakota, and Mount Rushmore. DB: Answers will vary.

Page 12

Draw lines to match company/Co., boulevard/Blvd., street/St., avenue/Ave., road/Rd., United States of America/USA, and doctor/Dr.
RW: Answers will vary. DB Answers will vary.

Page 13

Draw lines to match days and months with their correct abbreviations. Rewrite sentences without abbreviations.
RW: Underline Cindy, Vine Street, lessons, Monday, Wednesday, Friday, months, Michigan, December, January, and February with yellow. DB: Answers will vary.

Page 14

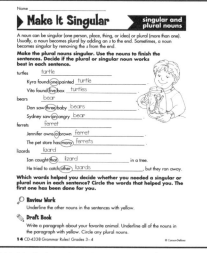

Make It Singular — singular and plural nouns

A noun can be singular (one person, place, thing, or idea) or plural (more than one). Usually, a noun becomes plural by adding an s to the end. Sometimes, a noun becomes singular by removing the s from the end.
Make the plural nouns singular. Use the nouns to finish the sentences. Decide if the plural or singular noun works best in each sentence.

turtles
Kyra found one painted turtle
Vito found five box turtles

bears
Dan saw three baby bears
Sydney saw an angry bear

ferrets
Jennifer owns a brown ferret
The pet store has many ferrets

lizards
Ian caught that lizard in a tree.
He tried to catch other lizards, but they ran away.

Which words helped you decide whether you needed a singular or plural noun in each sentence? Circle the words that helped you. The first one has been done for you.

Review Work
Underline the other nouns in the sentences with yellow.

Draft Book
Write a paragraph about your favorite animal. Underline all of the nouns in the paragraph with yellow. Circle any plural nouns.

14 CD-4338 Grammar Rules! Grades 3–4 © Carson-Dellosa

RW: Underline Kyra, Vito, Dan, Sydney, Jennifer, store, and Ian with yellow.
DB: Answers will vary.

Page 15

Sports — plural nouns

A noun can be singular (one person, place, thing, or idea) or plural (more than one). Usually, a noun becomes plural by adding an s to the end.
Make the nouns plural.

skate	skates	club	clubs
base	bases	racket	rackets
hurdle	hurdles	guard	guards
helmet	helmets	uniform	uniforms

Use the plural nouns to finish the sentences.

Jackie and Mario need their rackets to play tennis.
Delaney needs shin guards to play soccer.
Bobby got new hockey skates for his birthday.
The team's softball uniforms are blue.
The football players' helmets protected their heads.
Ling ran the bases after she hit a home run.
Willie wants his own set of golf clubs.
Brian jumped over the hurdles during track practice.

Review Work
Underline the other nouns in the sentences with yellow.

Draft Book
Write a paragraph about your favorite sport. Underline all of the nouns in the paragraph with yellow.

© Carson-Dellosa CD-4338 Grammar Rules! Grades 3–4 15

RW: Underline Jackie, Mario, tennis, Delaney, soccer, Bobby, team's, birthday, players', heads, Ling, home run, Willie, set, Brian, and practice with yellow.
DB: Answers will vary.

Critters — plural nouns

A noun can be singular (one person, place, thing, or idea) or plural (more than one). Sometimes, a noun becomes plural by adding *es* to the end.
example: crutch → crutches   example: class → classes
example: dish → dishes   example: box → boxes

Make the nouns plural.

lunch	lunches	dash	dashes
pouch	pouches	crunch	crunches
dress	dresses	brush	brushes
finch	finches	tax	taxes
fox	foxes	branch	branches

Use some of the plural nouns to finish the sentences.

My dad packed __lunches__ for my brother and me.

There are three __brushes__ on the bathroom counter.

Kangaroos, opossums, and koalas use their __pouches__ to carry their young.

The __branches__ of the tree were filled with __finches__ building nests.

🔍 **Review Work**
Underline the other nouns in the sentences with yellow.

✎ **Draft Book**
Make a list of nouns that become plural by adding *es* to the end of each. Start with the words on this page. Write the singular and plural forms of the words. Use these nouns in future writings.

16 CD-4338 Grammar Rules! Grades 3–4   © Carson-Dellosa

RW: Underline dad, brother, counter, kangaroos, opossums, koalas, young, tree, and nests with yellow. DB: Answers will vary.

Page 17

Different Endings — plural nouns

A noun can be singular (one person, place, thing, or idea) or plural (more than one). Usually, a noun becomes plural by adding an *s* to the end. A noun that ends with *ch*, *s*, *z*, *sh*, or *x* becomes plural by adding *es* to the end. A noun that ends with *f* or *fe* becomes plural by changing the *f* or *fe* to *v* and adding *es* to the end.
example: calf → calves   example: scarf → scarves

Make the nouns plural.

leaf	leaves	coach	coaches
half	halves	knife	knives
bench	benches	bunch	bunches
glass	glasses	lunch	lunches

Write the other form of each noun.

Red, yellow, and orange __leaves/leaf__ are falling from the trees.

Please put the __dishes/dish__, __glasses/glass__, __knives/knife__, and __forks/fork__ on the table.

For __lunch/lunches__, Jenna had two __halves/half__ of a sandwich and a __bunch/bunches__ of __grapes/grape__.

🔍 **Review Work**
Draw a star above each singular noun in the sentences.

✎ **Draft Book**
Two of the plural nouns were not used in the sentences. Write a sentence with each word. Underline the nouns with yellow.

CD-4338 Grammar Rules! Grades 3–4   **17**

RW: Draw a star above table, lunch, Jenna, sandwich, and bunch. DB: Answers will vary.

Page 18

Here Come the Ys — plural nouns

A noun can be singular (one person, place, thing, or idea) or plural (more than one). There are two rules for making a noun that ends with *y* plural. For a noun that ends with a consonant + *y*, change the *y* to *i* and add *es* to the end. For a noun that ends with a vowel + *y*, add an *s* to the end.
example: lady → ladies   example: toy → toys

Make the nouns plural.

Tonya has seventeen __guppies/guppy__ in her aquarium.

Did you forget your house __keys/key__ again?

Sometimes raccoons climb into __chimneys/chimney__ to make nests.

How many __pennies/penny__ do you have in your bank?

Wild __turkeys/turkey__ live in the woods by Jon's house.

Hal loves to have __strawberries/strawberry__ on his ice cream.

Gerald has read many __stories/story__ about ants.

__Monkeys/monkey__ living in the rain forests.

🔍 **Review Work**
Underline the other nouns in the sentences with yellow. Draw a star above each singular noun.

✎ **Draft Book**
Make these nouns plural: baby, pony, boy, and cherry. Use the plural nouns to write four sentences. Circle the plural nouns. Draw a star above each singular noun. __babies, ponies, boys, cherries__

18 CD-4338 Grammar Rules! Grades 3–4   © Carson-Dellosa

RW: Underline Tonya, aquarium, raccoons, nests, bank, woods, house, Hal, ice cream, Gerald, and rain forests with yellow. Draw a star above Tonya, aquarium, bank, house, Hal, ice cream, and Gerald. DB: Answers will vary.

Page 19

Make Mine Plural — plural nouns

A noun can be singular (one person, place, thing, or idea) or plural (more than one).
Make the nouns plural.

mess	messes		hobby	hobbies
wish	wishes		thief	thieves
wife	wives		donkey	donkeys
peach	peaches		daisy	daisies
dog	dogs		mass	masses
way	ways		rash	rashes
berry	berries		ray	rays
life	lives		baby	babies
crash	crashes		sky	skies
toy	toys		watch	watches
shelf	shelves		bay	bays
class	classes		candy	candies
elf	elves		day	days

🔍 **Review Work**
Write each singular noun from above that ends with *y* but does not have *es* when it is made plural.
__way, toy, donkey, ray, bay, day__

✎ **Draft Book**
Choose five pairs of nouns (singular and plural forms). Write a sentence with each noun.

© Carson-Dellosa   CD-4338 Grammar Rules! Grades 3–4   **19**

DB: Answers will vary.

Page 20

Draw lines to match ox/oxen, tooth/teeth, child/children, foot/feet, person/people, octopus/octopuses, man/men, woman/women, and bus/buses. Circle children, buses, octopuses, people, teeth, deer, sheep, men, series, women, and feet. RW: Underline aquarium, creatures, animals, zoo, tickets, playoffs, and race. DB: Answers will vary.

Page 21

Mine, All Mine — possessive nouns

A possessive noun shows belonging. If a noun is singular or if it is plural but does not end with an *s*, add an apostrophe + *s* ('s) to the end to make it possessive.
examples: cat's food, boss's pen, men's shoes
If a noun is plural and already ends with an *s*, add an apostrophe to the end.
examples: cats' collars, players' helmets

Finish each sentence with a possessive noun.

The pond belongs to those frogs. It is the __frogs'__ pond.

The crayons belong to Margaret. They are __Margaret's__ crayons.

The bats belong to those boys. They are the __boys'__ bats.

The swing belongs to Morris. It is __Morris's__ swing.

The hill belongs to the ants. It is the __ants'__ hill.

The hat belongs to Max. It is __Max's__ hat.

Those marbles belong to Louis. They are __Louis's__ marbles.

Make the nouns possessive.

girls	girls'	Chris	Chris's
frog	frog's	Jordan	Jordan's
dogs	dogs'	classmates	classmates'
women	women's	Mr. Moss	Mr. Moss's
Tito	Tito's	birds	birds'
teachers	teachers'	turtle	turtle's

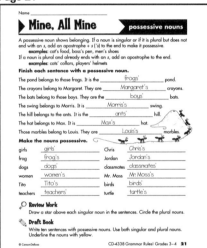

🔍 **Review Work**
Draw a star above each singular noun in the sentences. Circle the plural nouns.

✎ **Draft Book**
Write ten sentences with possessive nouns. Use both singular and plural nouns. Underline the nouns with yellow.

© Carson-Dellosa   CD-4338 Grammar Rules! Grades 3–4   **21**

RW: Draw a star above pond, pond, Margaret, swing, Morris, swing, hill, hill, hat, Max, hat, and Louis. Circle frogs, crayons, crayons, bats, boys, bats, ants, marbles, marbles. DB: Answers will vary.

Page 22

Who Owns It? — possessive nouns

A possessive noun shows belonging. If a noun is singular or if it is plural but does not end with an *s*, add an apostrophe + *s* ('s) to the end to make it possessive.
examples: cat's food, boss's pen, men's shoes
If a noun is plural and already ends with an *s*, add an apostrophe to the end.
examples: cats' collars, players' helmets

Circle the possessive noun in each sentence. How many people or things possess something? Circle 1 if one person or thing possesses something. Circle 2+ if more than one person or thing possesses something.

1	2+	The audience laughed at the (comedian's) performance.
1	2+	The (turtles') pond needs a log in it.
1	2+	The (dancer's) shoes had holes in them.
1	2+	A (book's) pages must be treated gently.
1	2+	The (chipmunks') home is stuffed with bird seed.
1	2+	Can you sharpen the (students') pencils?
1	2+	The (museum's) admission price is $3.00.
1	2+	Liz let (Craig's) five birds out of their cages.
1	2+	The (bluebird's) nest has three eggs.
1	2+	Hakim borrowed the (team's) score book.
1	2+	Sandra washed her (parents') cars.
1	2+	(Omar's) cat scratched me.

🔍 **Review Work**
Underline the other nouns in the sentences with yellow.

✎ **Draft Book**
Choose four friends. Use possessive nouns to write sentences about things that belong to them. Write two sentences about each friend.

22 CD-4338 Grammar Rules! Grades 3–4   © Carson-Dellosa

RW: Underline audience, performance, pond, log, shoes, holes, pages, home, seed, pencils, price, Liz, birds, cages, nest, eggs, Hakim, book, Sandra, cars, audience, and cat with yellow.
DB: Answers will vary.

Page 23

Hide-and-Seek — action verbs

An action verb tells what someone or something is doing.
example: The boy swings the golf club.
example: The mouse scampers across the floor.
Circle each action verb.

Waldo (hides) from his friend.

Marshall (searches) for the others.

Jane (crouches) behind the slide.

Sam (crawls) along the fence.

Sal (jumps) over the log.

Insects (scatter) out of the way.

Evelyn (giggles) behind the oak tree.

Joey (climbs) up the old maple.

The leaves on the old maple (sway) in the breeze.

Marshall (finds) Karen.

Karen (races) to the free spot.

Marshall (tags) Karen.

Karen (yells) for everyone to come out.

🔍 **Review Work**
Underline the nouns in the sentences with yellow.

✎ **Draft Book**
Find a page in your draft book with the nouns underlined with yellow. Underline the verbs with blue.

© Carson-Dellosa   CD-4338 Grammar Rules! Grades 3–4   **23**

RW: Underline Waldo, friend, Marshall, others, Jane, slide, Sam, fence, Sal, log, insects, way, Evelyn, tree, Joey, maple, leaves, maple, breeze, Marshall, Karen, Karen, spot, Marshall, Karen, and Karen with yellow.
DB: Answers will vary.

© Carson-Dellosa

CD-4338 Grammar Rules! Grades 3–4   **117**

Page 24 worksheet

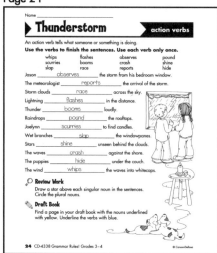

Thunderstorm — action verbs

An action verb tells what someone or something is doing.
Use the verbs to finish the sentences. Use each verb only once.

whips · flashes · observes · pound
scurries · booms · crash · shine
slap · race · reports · hide

Jason _observes_ the storm from his bedroom window.
The meteorologist _reports_ the arrival of the storm.
Storm clouds _race_ across the sky.
Lightning _flashes_ in the distance.
Thunder _booms_ loudly.
Raindrops _pound_ the rooftops.
Joelynn _scurries_ to find candles.
Wet branches _slap_ the windowpanes.
Stars _shine_ unseen behind the clouds.
The waves _crash_ against the shore.
The puppies _hide_ under the couch.
The wind _whips_ the waves into whitecaps.

Review Work
Draw a star above each singular noun in the sentences. Circle the plural nouns.

Draft Book
Find a page in your draft book with the nouns underlined with yellow. Underline the verbs with blue.

24 CD-4338 Grammar Rules! Grades 3–4

RW: Draw a star above Jason, storm, window, meteorologist, arrival, storm, sky, lightning, distance, thunder, Joelynn, shore, couch, and wind. Circle clouds, raindrops, rooftops, candles, branches, windowpanes, stars, clouds, waves, puppies, waves, and whitecaps.
DB: Answers will vary.

Page 25 worksheet

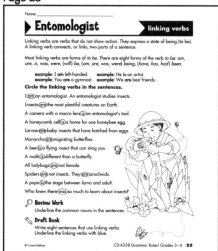

Entomologist — linking verbs

Linking verbs are verbs that do not show action. They express a state of being (to be). A linking verb connects, or links, two parts of a sentence.

Most linking verbs are forms of to be. There are eight forms of the verb to be: am, are, is, was, were, (will) be, (am, are, was, were) being, (have, has, had) been.

example: I am left-handed. **example:** He is an artist.
example: You are a gymnast. **example:** We are best friends.
Circle the linking verbs in the sentences.

I _am_ an entomologist. An entomologist studies insects.
Insects _are_ the most plentiful creatures on Earth.
A camera with a macro lens _is_ an entomologist's tool.
A honeycomb cell _is_ a home for one honeybee egg.
Larvae _are_ baby insects that have hatched from eggs.
Monarchs _are_ migrating butterflies.
A bee _is_ a flying insect that can sting you.
A moth _is_ different than a butterfly.
All ladybugs _are_ not female.
Spiders _are_ not insects. They _are_ arachnids.
A pupa _is_ the stage between larva and adult.
Who knew there _was_ so much to learn about insects?

Review Work
Underline the common nouns in the sentences.

Draft Book
Write eight sentences that use linking verbs. Underline the linking verbs with blue.

CD-4338 Grammar Rules! Grades 3–4 25

RW: Underline entomologist, entomologist, insects, insects, creatures, camera, lens, tool, cell, home, egg, larvae, insects, eggs, monarchs, butterflies, bee, insect, moth, butterfly, ladybugs, female, spiders, insects, arachnids, pupa, stage, larva, adult, and insects. DB: Answers will vary.

Page 26 worksheet

Link Them Together — linking verbs

Linking verbs are verbs that do not show action. They express a state of being. A linking verb connects, or links, two parts of an action verb.

Most linking verbs are forms of to be. There are eight forms of the verb to be: am, are, is, was, were, (will) be, (am, are, was, were) being, (have, has, had) been.
Circle the linking verbs in the sentences.

Rena _was_ in the gym.
The garbage cans _were_ full.
Hannah _will be_ in second grade next year.
We _have been_ patient.
Shane and James _had been_ sick with the flu.
Those gray birds in that tree _are being_ very noisy.
The picture above the door _is_ one that I painted.
Matches _are_ dangerous.
I _am_ careful near the baby.
Carol's hair _is_ very short.
Richard _has been_ asleep all afternoon.
The dinosaur fossils _were_ very interesting.

Review Work
Underline the common nouns in the sentences. Draw an X next to each proper noun that names a person. Draw a check next to the possessive noun.

Draft Book
Write eight sentences that use linking verbs. Use a variety of the verbs from this page. Underline the linking verbs with blue.

26 CD-4338 Grammar Rules! Grades 3–4

RW: Underline gym, cans, grade, year, flu, birds, tree, picture, door, matches, baby, hair, afternoon, and fossils. Draw an X next to Rena, Hannah, Shane, James, Carol, and Richard. Draw a check next to Carol's. DB: Answers will vary.

Page 27 worksheet

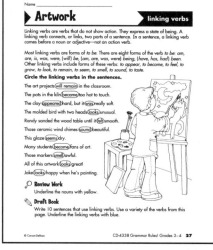

Artwork — linking verbs

Linking verbs are verbs that do not show action. They express a state of being. A linking verb connects, or links, two parts of a sentence. In a sentence, a linking verb comes before a noun or adjective—not an action verb.

Most linking verbs are forms of the verb to be: am, are, is, was, were, (will) be, (am, are, was, were) being, (have, has, had) been. Other linking verbs include forms of these verbs: (will) be, (am, to become, to feel, to grow, to look, to remain, to seem, to smell, to sound, to taste.
Circle the linking verbs in the sentences.

The art projects _will remain_ in the classroom.
The pots in the kiln _became_ too hot to touch.
The clay _appeared_ hard, but it _was_ really soft.
The molded bird with two heads _looks_ unusual.
Randy sanded the wood table until it _felt_ smooth.
Those ceramic wind chimes _sound_ beautiful.
This glaze _seems_ dry.
Many students _become_ fans of art.
Those markers _smell_ awful.
All of this artwork _looks_ great!
Jake _looks_ happy when he's painting.

Review Work
Underline the nouns with yellow.

Draft Book
Write 10 sentences that use linking verbs. Use a variety of the verbs from this page. Underline the linking verbs with blue.

CD-4338 Grammar Rules! Grades 3–4 27

RW: Underline projects, classroom, pots, kiln, clay, bird, heads, Randy, table, chimes, glaze, students, art, markers, artwork, and Jake with yellow. DB: Answers will vary.

Page 28 worksheet

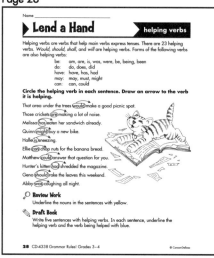

Lend a Hand — helping verbs

Helping verbs are verbs that help main verbs express tenses. There are 23 helping verbs. Would, should, shall, and will are helping verbs. Forms of the following verbs are also helping verbs:
be: am, are, is, was, were, be, being, been
do: do, does, did
have: have, has, had
may: may, must, might
can: can, could

Circle the helping verb in each sentence. Draw an arrow to the verb it is helping.

That area under the trees _would_ make a good picnic spot.
Those crickets _are_ making a lot of noise.
Melissa _has_ eaten her sandwich already.
Quinn _might_ buy a new bike.
Halle _is_ sneezing.
Ellie _can_ chop nuts for the banana bread.
Matthew _could_ answer that question for you.
Hunter's kitten _had_ shredded the magazine.
Geno _should_ rake the leaves this weekend.
Abby _was_ coughing all night.

Review Work
Underline the nouns in the sentences with yellow.

Draft Book
Write five sentences with helping verbs. In each sentence, underline the helping verb and the verb being helped with blue.

28 CD-4338 Grammar Rules! Grades 3–4

Page 28 (cont.)
RW: Underline area, trees, spot, crickets, noise, Melissa, sandwich, Quinn, bike, Halle, Ellie, nuts, bread, Matthew, question, Hunter's, kitten, magazine, Geno, leaves, weekend, Abby, and night with yellow.
DB: Answers will vary.

Page 29 worksheet

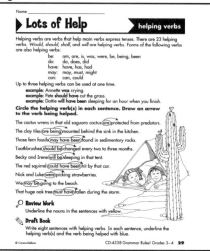

Lots of Help — helping verbs

Helping verbs are verbs that help main verbs tenses. There are 23 helping verbs. Would, should, shall, and will are helping verbs. Forms of the following verbs are also helping verbs:
be: am, are, is, was, were, be, being, been
do: do, does, did
have: have, has, had
may: may, must, might
can: can, could
Up to three helping verbs can be used at one time.
example: Annette was crying.
example: Pete should have cut the grass.
example: Dottie will have been sleeping for an hour when you finish.
Circle the helping verb(s) in each sentence. Draw an arrow to the verb being helped.

The cactus wrens in that old saguaro cactus _are_ protected from predators.
The clay tiles _are being_ mounted behind the sink in the kitchen.
Those fern fossils _may have been_ found in sedimentary rocks.
Toothbrushes _should be_ changed every two to three months.
Becky and Irene _will be_ sleeping in that tent.
The red squirrel _could have been_ hit by that car.
Nick and Luke _were_ picking strawberries.
We _may be_ going to the beach.
That huge oak tree _must have_ fallen during the storm.

Review Work
Underline the nouns in the sentences with yellow.

Draft Book
Write eight sentences with helping verbs. In each sentence, underline the helping verb(s) and the verb being helped with blue.

CD-4338 Grammar Rules! Grades 3–4 29

RW: Underline wrens, cactus, predators, tiles, sink, kitchen, fossils, rocks, toothbrushes, months, Becky, Irene, tent, squirrel, car, Nick, Luke, strawberries, beach, tree, and storm with yellow. DB: Answers will vary.

Page 30: Answers will vary.

Page 31 worksheet

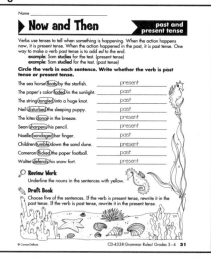

Now and Then — past and present tense

Verbs use tenses to tell when something is happening. When the action happens now, it is present tense. When the action happened in the past, it is past tense. One way to make a verb past tense is to add ed to the end.
example: Sam studies for the test. (present tense)
example: Sam studied for the test. (past tense)
Circle the verb in each sentence. Write whether the verb is past tense or present tense.

The sea horse _floats_ by the starfish. — present
The paper's color _faded_ in the sunlight. — past
The string _tangled_ into a huge knot. — past
Neil _disturbed_ the sleeping puppy. — past
The kites _dance_ in the breeze. — present
Sean _sharpens_ his pencil. — present
Noelle _bandaged_ her finger. — past
Children _tumble_ down the sand dune. — present
Cameron _flicked_ the paper football. — past
Walter _defends_ his snow fort. — present

Review Work
Underline the nouns in the sentences with yellow.

Draft Book
Choose five of the sentences. If the verb is present tense, rewrite it in the past tense. If the verb is past tense, rewrite it in the present tense.

CD-4338 Grammar Rules! Grades 3–4 31

RW: Underline sea horse, starfish, color, sunlight, string, knot, Neil, puppy, kites, breeze, Sean, pencil, Noelle, finger, children, dune, Cameron, football, Walter, and fort with yellow. DB: Answers will vary.

Answer Key

Page 32

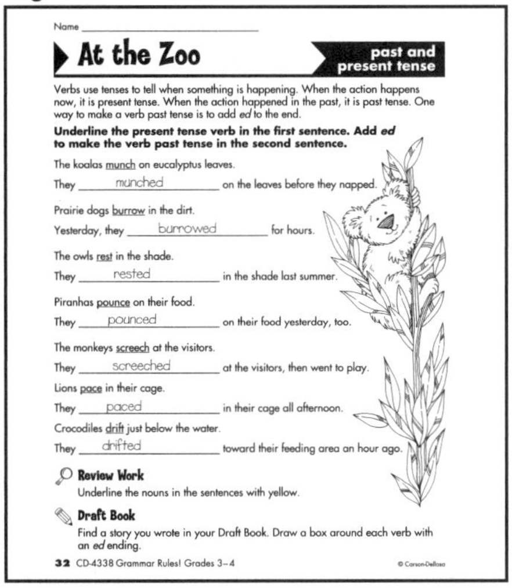

Name ____________________

At the Zoo — past and present tense

Verbs use tenses to tell when something is happening. When the action happens now, it is present tense. When the action happened in the past, it is past tense. One way to make a verb past tense is to add *ed* to the end.

Underline the present tense verb in the first sentence. Add *ed* to make the verb past tense in the second sentence.

The koalas munch on eucalyptus leaves.
They munched on the leaves before they napped.
Prairie dogs burrow in the dirt.
Yesterday, they burrowed for hours.
The owls rest in the shade.
They rested in the shade last summer.
Piranhas pounce on their food.
They pounced on their food yesterday, too.
The monkeys screech at the visitors.
They screeched at the visitors, then went to play.
Lions pace in their cage.
They paced in their cage all afternoon.
Crocodiles drift just below the water.
They drifted toward their feeding area an hour ago.

Review Work
Underline the nouns in the sentences with yellow.

Draft Book
Find a story you wrote in your Draft Book. Draw a box around each verb with an *ed* ending.

32 CD-4338 Grammar Rules! Grades 3–4 © Carson-Dellosa

RW: Underline koalas, leaves, leaves, prairie dogs, dirt, hours, owls, shade, shade, summer, piranhas, food, food, monkeys, visitors, visitors, lions, cage, cage, afternoon, crocodiles, water, area, and hour with yellow.
DB: Answers will vary.

Page 33

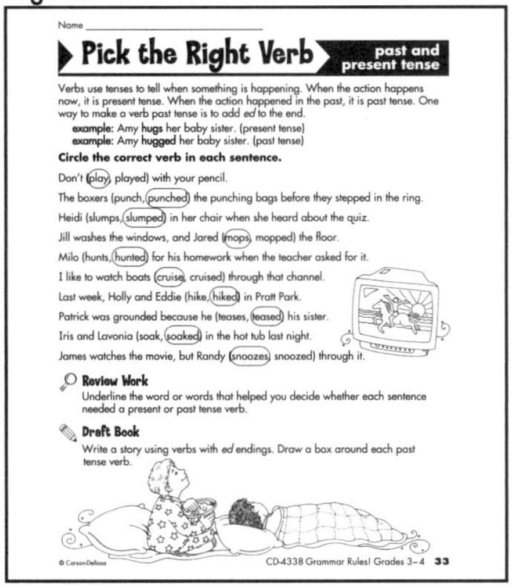

Name ____________________

Pick the Right Verb — past and present tense

Verbs use tenses to tell when something is happening. When the action happens now, it is present tense. When the action happened in the past, it is past tense. One way to make a verb past tense is to add *ed* to the end.
example: Amy **hugs** her baby sister. (present tense)
example: Amy **hugged** her baby sister. (past tense)

Circle the correct verb in each sentence.

Don't (play, played) with your pencil.
The boxers (punch, punched) the punching bags before they stepped in the ring.
Heidi (slumps, slumped) in her chair when she heard about the quiz.
Jill washes the windows, and Jared (mops, mopped) the floor.
Milo (hunts, hunted) for his homework when the teacher asked for it.
I like to watch boats (cruise, cruised) through that channel.
Last week, Holly and Eddie (hike, hiked) in Pratt Park.
Patrick was grounded because he (teases, teased) his sister.
Iris and Lavonia (soak, soaked) in the hot tub last night.
James watches the movie, but Randy (snoozes, snoozed) through it.

Review Work
Underline the word or words that helped you decide whether each sentence needed a present or past tense verb.

Draft Book
Write a story using verbs with *ed* endings. Draw a box around each past tense verb.

© Carson-Dellosa CD-4338 Grammar Rules! Grades 3–4 33

RW: Underline don't, stepped, heard, washes, asked, watch, last week, was grounded, last night, and watches. DB: Answers will vary.

Page 34

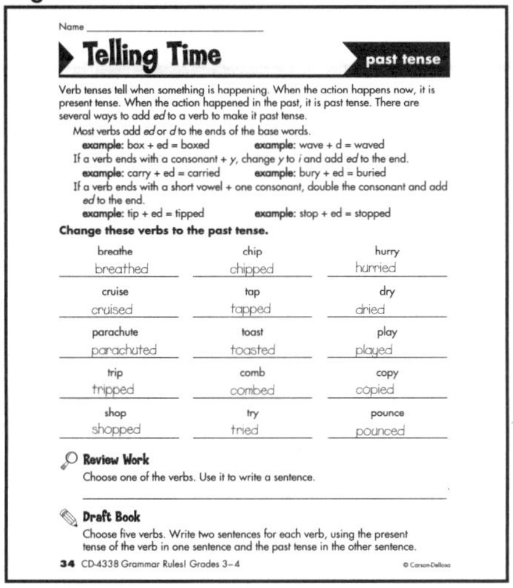

Name ____________________

Telling Time — past tense

Verb tenses tell when something is happening. When the action happens now, it is present tense. When the action happened in the past, it is past tense. There are several ways to add *ed* to a verb to make it past tense.
Most verbs add *ed* or *d* to the ends of the base words.
example: box + ed = boxed **example:** wave + d = waved
If a verb ends with a consonant + *y*, change *y* to *i* and add *ed* to the end.
example: carry + ed = carried **example:** bury + ed = buried
If a verb ends with a short vowel + one consonant, double the consonant and add *ed* to the end.
example: tip + ed = tipped **example:** stop + ed = stopped

Change these verbs to the past tense.

breathe — breathed	chip — chipped	hurry — hurried
cruise — cruised	tap — tapped	dry — dried
parachute — parachuted	toast — toasted	play — played
trip — tripped	comb — combed	copy — copied
shop — shopped	try — tried	pounce — pounced

Review Work
Choose one of the verbs. Use it to write a sentence.

Draft Book
Choose five verbs. Write two sentences for each verb, using the present tense of the verb in one sentence and the past tense in the other sentence.

34 CD-4338 Grammar Rules! Grades 3–4 © Carson-Dellosa

Page 34 (cont.)

RW: Answers will vary. DB: Answers will vary.

Page 35

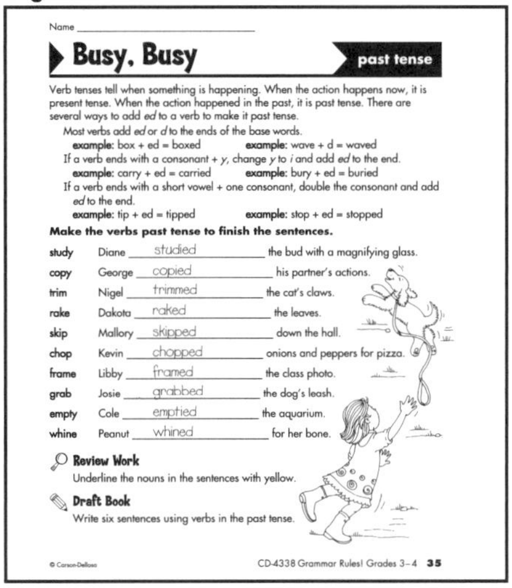

Name ____________________

Busy, Busy — past tense

Verb tenses tell when something is happening. When the action happens now, it is present tense. When the action happened in the past, it is past tense. There are several ways to add *ed* to a verb to make it past tense.
Most verbs add *ed* or *d* to the ends of the base words.
example: box + ed = boxed **example:** wave + d = waved
If a verb ends with a consonant + *y*, change *y* to *i* and add *ed* to the end.
example: carry + ed = carried **example:** bury + ed = buried
If a verb ends with a short vowel + one consonant, double the consonant and add *ed* to the end.
example: tip + ed = tipped **example:** stop + ed = stopped

Make the verbs past tense to finish the sentences.

study Diane studied the bud with a magnifying glass.
copy George copied his partner's actions.
trim Nigel trimmed the cat's claws.
rake Dakota raked the leaves.
skip Mallory skipped down the hall.
chop Kevin chopped onions and peppers for pizza.
frame Libby framed the class photo.
grab Josie grabbed the dog's leash.
empty Cole emptied the aquarium.
whine Peanut whined for her bone.

Review Work
Underline the nouns in the sentences with yellow.

Draft Book
Write six sentences using verbs in the past tense.

© Carson-Dellosa CD-4338 Grammar Rules! Grades 3–4 35

RW: Underline Diane, bud, magnifying glass, George, partner's, actions, Nigel, cat's, claws, Dakota, leaves, Mallory, hall, Kevin, onions, peppers, pizza, Libby, photo, Josie, dog's, leash, Cole, aquarium, Peanut, and bone with yellow.
DB: Answers will vary.

Page 36

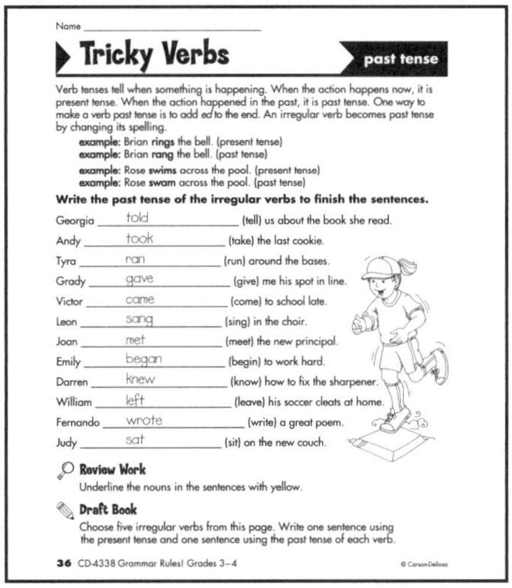

Name ____________________

Tricky Verbs — past tense

Verb tenses tell when something is happening. When the action happens now, it is present tense. When the action happened in the past, it is past tense. One way to make a verb past tense is to add *ed* to the end. An irregular verb becomes past tense by changing its spelling.
example: Brian **rings** the bell. (present tense)
example: Brian **rang** the bell. (past tense)
example: Rose **swims** across the pool. (present tense)
example: Rose **swam** across the pool. (past tense)

Write the past tense of the irregular verbs to finish the sentences.

Georgia told (tell) us about the book she read.
Andy took (take) the last cookie.
Tyra ran (run) around the bases.
Grady gave (give) me his spot in line.
Victor came (come) to school late.
Leon sang (sing) in the choir.
Joan met (meet) the new principal.
Emily began (begin) to work hard.
Darren knew (know) how to fix the sharpener.
William left (leave) his soccer cleats at home.
Fernando wrote (write) a great poem.
Judy sat (sit) on the new couch.

Review Work
Underline the nouns in the sentences with yellow.

Draft Book
Choose five irregular verbs from this page. Write one sentence using the present tense and one sentence using the past tense of each verb.

36 CD-4338 Grammar Rules! Grades 3–4 © Carson-Dellosa

RW: Underline Georgia, book, Andy, cookie, Tyra, bases, Grady, spot, line, Victor, school, Leon, choir, Joan, principal, Emily, Darren, sharpener, William, cleats, home, Fernando, poem, Judy, and couch with yellow.
DB: Answers will vary.

Page 37

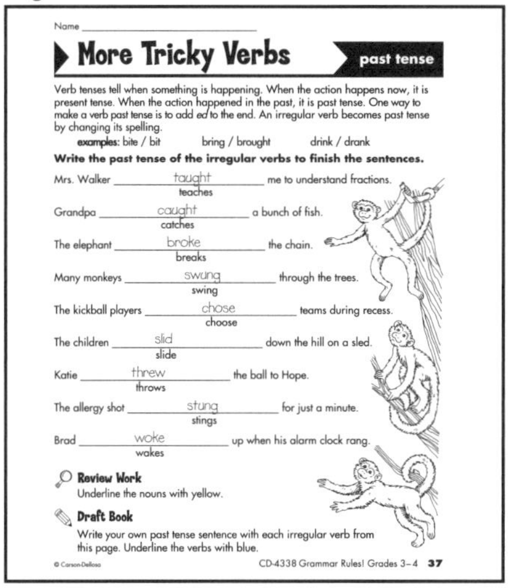

Name ____________________

More Tricky Verbs — past tense

Verb tenses tell when something is happening. When the action happens now, it is present tense. When the action happened in the past, it is past tense. One way to make a verb past tense is to add *ed* to the end. An irregular verb becomes past tense by changing its spelling.
examples: bite / bit bring / brought drink / drank

Write the past tense of the irregular verbs to finish the sentences.

Mrs. Walker taught (teaches) me to understand fractions.
Grandpa caught (catches) a bunch of fish.
The elephant broke (breaks) the chain.
Many monkeys swung (swing) through the trees.
The kickball players chose (choose) teams during recess.
The children slid (slide) down the hill on a sled.
Katie threw (throws) the ball to Hope.
The allergy shot stung (stings) for just a minute.
Brad woke (wakes) up when his alarm clock rang.

Review Work
Underline the nouns with yellow.

Draft Book
Write your own past tense sentence with each irregular verb from this page. Underline the verbs with blue.

© Carson-Dellosa CD-4338 Grammar Rules! Grades 3–4 37

RW: Underline Mrs. Walker, fractions, Grandpa, fish, elephant, chain, monkeys, trees, players, teams, recess, children, hill, sled, Katie, ball, Hope, shot, minute, Brad, and alarm clock with yellow. DB: Answers will vary.

Page 38

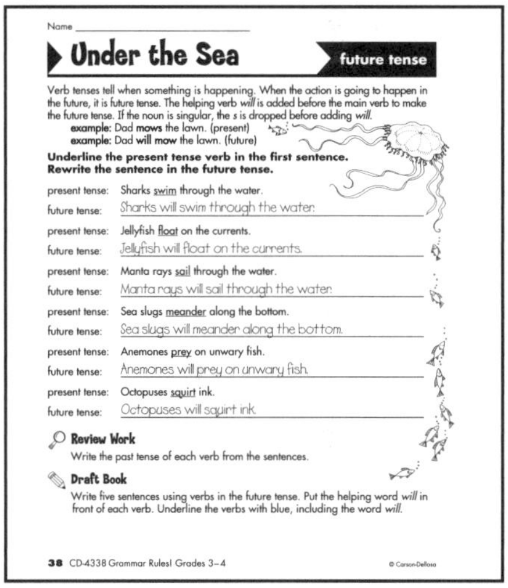

Name ____________________

Under the Sea — future tense

Verb tenses tell when something is happening. When the action is going to happen in the future, it is future tense. The helping verb *will* is added before the main verb to make the future tense. If the noun is singular, the *s* is dropped before adding *will*.
example: Dad **mows** the lawn. (present)
example: Dad **will mow** the lawn. (future)

Underline the present tense verb in the first sentence. Rewrite the sentence in the future tense.

present tense: Sharks swim through the water.
future tense: Sharks will swim through the water.
present tense: Jellyfish float on the currents.
future tense: Jellyfish will float on the currents.
present tense: Manta rays sail through the water.
future tense: Manta rays will sail through the water.
present tense: Sea slugs meander along the bottom.
future tense: Sea slugs will meander along the bottom.
present tense: Anemones prey on unwary fish.
future tense: Anemones will prey on unwary fish.
present tense: Octopuses squirt ink.
future tense: Octopuses will squirt ink.

Review Work
Write the past tense of each verb from the sentences.

Draft Book
Write five sentences using verbs in the future tense. Put the helping word *will* in front of each verb. Underline the verbs with blue, including the word *will*.

38 CD-4338 Grammar Rules! Grades 3–4 © Carson-Dellosa

RW: Write swam, floated, sailed, meandered, preyed, and squirted. DB: Answers will vary.

Page 39

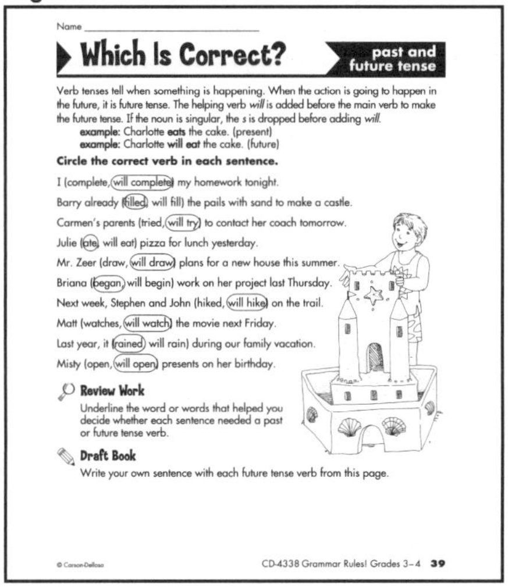

Name ____________________

Which Is Correct? — past and future tense

Verb tenses tell when something is happening. When the action is going to happen in the future, it is future tense. The helping verb *will* is added before the main verb to make the future tense. If the noun is singular, the *s* is dropped before adding *will*.
example: Charlotte **eats** the cake. (present)
example: Charlotte **will eat** the cake. (future)

Circle the correct verb in each sentence.

I (complete, will complete) my homework tonight.
Barry already (filled, will fill) the pails with sand to make a castle.
Carmen's parents (tried, will try) to contact her coach tomorrow.
Julie (ate, will eat) pizza for lunch yesterday.
Mr. Zeer (draw, will draw) plans for a new house this summer.
Briana (began, will begin) work on her project last Thursday.
Next week, Stephen and John (hiked, will hike) on the trail.
Matt (watches, will watch) the movie next Friday.
Last year, it (rained, will rain) during our family vacation.
Misty (open, will open) presents on her birthday.

Review Work
Underline the word or words that helped you decide whether each sentence needed a past or future tense verb.

Draft Book
Write your own sentence with each future tense verb from this page.

© Carson-Dellosa CD-4338 Grammar Rules! Grades 3–4 39

Page 39 (cont.)
RW: Underline tonight, already, tomorrow, yesterday, this summer, last Thursday, next week, next Friday, last year, and on her birthday.
DB: Answers will vary.

Page 40

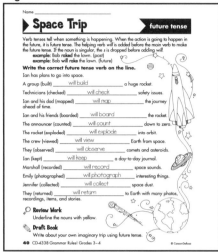

▶ **Space Trip** — future tense

Verb tenses tell when something is happening. When the action is going to happen in the future, it is future tense. The helping verb *will* is added before the main verb to make the future tense. If the noun is singular, the s is dropped before adding will.
example: Bob raked the lawn. (past)
Bob **will rake** the lawn. (future)
Write the correct future tense verb on the line.

Ian has plans to go into space.
A group (built) ___will build___ a huge rocket.
Technicians (checked) ___will check___ safety issues.
Ian and his dad (mapped) ___will map___ the journey ahead of time.
Ian and his friends (boarded) ___will board___ the rocket.
The announcer (counted) ___will count___ down to zero.
The rocket (exploded) ___will explode___ into orbit.
The crew (viewed) ___will view___ Earth from space.
They (observed) ___will observe___ comets and asteroids.
Ian (kept) ___will keep___ a day-to-day journal.
Marshall (recorded) ___will record___ space sounds.
Emily (photographed) ___will photograph___ interesting things.
Jennifer (collected) ___will collect___ space dust.
They (returned) ___will return___ to Earth with many photos, recordings, items, and stories.

Review Work
Underline the nouns with yellow.

Draft Book
Write about your own imaginary trip using future tense.

40 CD-4338 Grammar Rules! Grades 3–4

RW: Underline Ian, plans, space, group, rocket, technicians, issues, Ian, dad, journey, time, Ian, friends, rocket, announcer, zero, rocket, orbit, crew, Earth, space, comets, asteroids, Ian, journal, Marshall, sounds, Emily things, Jennifer, dust, Earth, photos, recordings, items, and stories with yellow.
DB: Answers will vary.

Page 41

▶ **Past, Present, or Future** — verb tenses

Verb tenses tell when something is happening.
Underline the verbs in the sentences. If the verb is future tense, underline both the main verb and the helping verb *will*. **Circle past, present, or future.**

Vanessa signed her name on the card.	past
Greg will golf in the tournament.	future
Maegen snaps the links together.	present
Brantley climbs into his bunk bed.	present
Layne will set her alarm clock.	future
Kallie rocked her puppy to sleep.	past
Jill will dip the strawberries in chocolate.	future
Raymond catches a line drive.	present
Jade calculated the answer.	past
Fran will input the test.	future
Lisa will prepare lunch.	future
Ryan pestered his mother.	past
Lori sealed the envelope.	past
Teresa will polish her fingernails.	future
Mike will spend the night at a friend's house.	future

Review Work
Underline the nouns with yellow.

Draft Book
Write two sentences for each verb tense. Underline the verbs with blue. Label the sentences past tense, present tense, or future tense.

CD-4338 Grammar Rules! Grades 3–4 41

RW: Underline Vanessa, name, card, Greg, tournament, Maegen, links, Brantley, bunk bed, Layne, alarm clock, Kallie, puppy, Jill, strawberries, chocolate, Raymond, line drive, Jade, answer, Fran, test, Lisa, lunch, Ryan, mother, Lori, envelope, Teresa, fingernails, Mike night, friend's, and house with yellow.
DB: Answers will vary.

Page 42

▶ **Not, Not, Not!** — contractions

A contraction is two words that are put together to form one word. Some of the letters drop out of the second word when the words are joined. An apostrophe replaces those letters.
The word *not* forms a contraction with many helping or linking verbs.
example: did + not = didn't
The contraction for *will not* is an exception: will + not = won't.
Add n't to the helping or linking verbs to make contractions.

are	aren't	is	isn't
was	wasn't	were	weren't
do	don't	does	doesn't
can	can't	had	hadn't
has	hasn't	should	shouldn't

Write a contraction for each sentence. Try to use each contraction only once.

Sharon and Jill ___don't/can't___ follow the directions.
Gerard ___didn't/doesn't___ canoe without a life jacket.
Antoine ___didn't/doesn't___ know how to cook.
Madalen ___wasn't/isn't___ very hungry.
Caleb ___hasn't/hadn't___ phoned me yet.
Maegen ___isn't/wasn't___ tired.
Mia ___hadn't___ cleaned the horse stall when I left.

Review Work
Find the other verbs in the sentences. Underline them with blue.

Draft Book
Choose six contractions. Write a sentence with each one.

42 CD-4338 Grammar Rules! Grades 3–4

RW: Underline follow, canoe, know, phoned, cleaned, and left with blue.
DB: Answers will vary.

Page 43

▶ **Throw Some Out** — contractions

A contraction is two words that are put together to form one word. Some of the letters drop out of the second word when the words are joined. An apostrophe replaces those letters. The following letters are left with the apostrophe when a contraction is made:

n't when you add *not* (isn't)   'll when you add *will* (she'll)
'd when you add *would* or *had* (we'd)   's when you add *is* or *has* (it's)
're when you add *are* (we're)   've when you add *have* (I've)

Combine the words to make contractions.

I + will =	I'll	he + is =	he's
they + are =	they're	they + have =	they've
he + will =	he'll	she + has =	she's
I + had =	I'd	they + would =	they'd
what + is =	what's	here + is =	here's
could + not =	couldn't	they + will =	they'll

Write the correct contraction on the line in each sentence.

Carter should not ___shouldn't___ ride his skateboard without a helmet.
Ariel did not ___didn't___ remember to do her homework.
That is the strongest thing I have ___I've___ ever seen!
Do you think they are ___they're___ coming to the game?
I think I will ___I'll___ buy a new backpack.
Who is ___Who's___ on the telephone?

Review Work
Underline the action verbs in the sentences with blue.

Draft Book
Choose eight contractions. Write a sentence with each one.

© Carson-Dellosa   CD-4338 Grammar Rules! Grades 3–4 43

RW: Underline ride, remember, seen, coming, and buy with blue. DB: Answers will vary.

Page 44

▶ **What We're Doing** — verb endings

A verb follows the same rules as a noun when adding s or es to the end.
Add s to the ends of most verbs.   **example:** run + s = runs
Add es to the end if the verb ends in sh, s, z, ch, or x.   **example:** pitch + es = pitches
Change y to i and add es to the end if the verb ends with a consonant + y.   **example:** try + es = tries
Add s to the end if the verb ends with a vowel + y.   **example:** enjoy + s = enjoys
Finish each sentence with the verb and its correct ending.

crunch Anna ___crunches___ on a carrot.
fly Amelia ___flies___ her kite.
toy Cody ___toys___ with his food.
fix Nell ___fixes___ her bicycle.
dish Ben ___dishes___ out the spaghetti.
play Vinny ___plays___ the piano.
buzz Paul ___buzzes___ like a bee.
teach Maria ___teaches___ her brother to tie his shoes.
finish Frank ___finishes___ his ice cream.
pass Ronald ___passes___ the football.
spy Wrenn ___spies___ on her friends.

Review Work
What kind of verb is used in each sentence? Circle the correct answer.
(action) linking helping

Draft Book
Write five sentences. Use singular nouns and verbs with the correct endings. Use the rules on this page.

44 CD-4338 Grammar Rules! Grades 3–4

DB: Answers will vary.

Page 45

▶ **Twilight** — noun and verb agreement

A singular noun uses a verb that has an s at the end.
example: The boy climbs the tree.
A plural noun uses a verb that does not have an s at the end.
example: The boys climb the tree.
Circle the correct verb(s) in each sentence.

Fluffy white clouds (drift) drifts along.
The sun (fade, (fades)) behind the horizon.
A dog (bound, (bounds)) into the yard.
The door (open, (opens)) opens.
The boy (hear, (hears)) many sounds.
Buddy (run, (runs)) into the woods and Calvin (follow, (follows)).
Calvin (walk, (walks)) out after his dog, Buddy.
Owls (call) calls to one another.
Insects (buzz) buzzes and (hum) hums.
Bullfrogs (croak) croaks.
The two friends (return) returns home in soft darkness.
Stars (twinkle) twinkles in the sky.
Calvin (call, (calls)) quietly to Buddy.
Buddy (reenter, (reenters)) the house with Calvin.

Review Work
Underline the nouns in the sentences with yellow.

Draft Book
Choose five of the sentences. Rewrite each one so that the first noun becomes the opposite (singular or plural) of what it is now. Make sure the verb has the correct ending to agree with the new noun.

CD-4338 Grammar Rules! Grades 3–4 45

RW: Underline clouds, sun, horizon, dog, yard, door, boy, sounds, Buddy, woods, Calvin, Calvin, dog, Buddy, owls, insects, bullfrogs, friends, home, darkness, stars, sky, Calvin, Buddy, Buddy, house, and Calvin with yellow.
DB: Answers will vary.

Page 46

▶ **How You Exercise** — noun and verb agreement

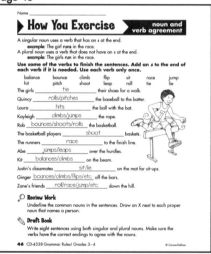

A singular noun uses a verb that has an s at the end.
example: The girl runs in the race.
A plural noun uses a verb that does not have an s at the end.
example: The girls run in the race.
Use some of the verbs to finish the sentences. Add an s to the end of each verb if it is needed. Use each verb only once.

balance bounce climb flip sit race jump
hit pitch shoot leap roll tie lie

The girls ___tie___ their shoes for a walk.
Quincy ___rolls/pitches___ the baseball to the batter.
Laura ___hits___ the ball with the bat.
Kayleigh ___climbs/jumps___ the rope.
Rob ___bounces/shoots/rolls___ the basketball.
The basketball players ___shoot___ baskets.
The runners ___race___ to the finish line.
Abe ___jumps/leaps___ over the hurdles.
Kit ___balances/climbs___ on the beam.
Justin's classmates ___sit/lie___ on the mat for sit-ups.
Ginger ___bounces/climbs/flips/etc.___ off the bars.
Zane's friends ___roll/race/jump/etc.___ down the hill.

Review Work
Underline the common nouns in the sentences. Draw an X next to each proper noun that names a person.

Draft Book
Write eight sentences using both singular and plural nouns. Make sure the verbs have the correct endings to agree with the nouns.

46 CD-4338 Grammar Rules! Grades 3–4

RW: Underline girls, shoes, walk, baseball, batter, ball, bat, rope, basketball, players, baskets, runners, finish line, hurdles, beam, classmates, mat, sit-ups, bars, friends, and hill. Draw an X next to Quincy, Laura, Kayleigh, Rob, Abe, Kit, Justin, Ginger, and Zane.
DB: Answers will vary.

Page 47

Five Senses — noun and verb agreement

A singular noun uses a verb that has an *s* at the end. A plural noun uses a verb that does not have an *s* at the end.

Choose the correct noun and verb to finish each sentence. Write the words on the lines.

The horse's ___teeth___ ___chomp___ the apple.
tooth / teeth   chomps / chomp

Sal's right ___eye___ ___sees___ better than his left eye.
eye / eyes   see / sees

Paul's left ___eyebrow___ ___lifts___ when he doesn't believe you.
eyebrow / eyebrows   lift / lifts

A rabbit's two long ___ears___ can ___hear___ a fox coming.
ear / ears   hear / hears

My ___nose___ ___smells___ something good.
nose / noses   smells / smell

Our ___mouths___ can ___taste___ freshly baked cookies.
mouth / mouths   taste / tastes

All of our ___toes___ ___wiggle___ in the sand.
toe / toes   wiggle / wiggles

The baby's five little ___fingers___ ___touch___ her cheek.
finger / fingers   touches / touch

Review Work
Underline the singular nouns in the sentences with yellow.

Draft Book
Write a story. Underline the nouns in the story with yellow. Underline the verbs with blue. Make sure your nouns and verbs agree.

© Carson-Dellosa   CD-4338 Grammar Rules! Grades 3–4   47

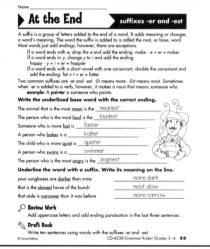

RW: Underline apple, eye, fox, sand, and cheek with yellow.
DB: Answers will vary.

Page 48

Describers — adjectives

Adjectives are words that describe nouns. Adjectives tell what kind, how many, or which one. They can include number, color, size, shape, or other detail words.
example: The *dirty* puppy needs a bath.
example: The *public* library is closed today.
A sentence can have more than one adjective: *Four, gray* bugs are in the *small* garden.

Circle the adjectives. Draw an arrow from the adjective to the noun it describes.

An *excited* Devon opened the *wrapped* package.
Many *tiny* ants crawled across the *jelly* sandwich.
A *bothersome* mosquito buzzes near my ear.
The *sweet, sticky* cotton candy is gone.
Walter has *dirty* socks and *muddy* shoes in that bag.
Four *spotted* dalmatians rode on the *noisy, red* fire engine.
Sal used the *sharp* scissors to cut the *thick, brown* paper.
Justin squeezed *two tan* lemons for lemonade.
Polly ate a *large, red* apple.
Zoe listened to the *jazz* music.

Review Work
Underline the nouns with yellow and the verbs with blue.

Draft Book
Write five sentences that have adjectives in them. Circle the adjectives. Draw an arrow from each adjective to the noun it describes.

48   CD-4338 Grammar Rules! Grades 3–4   © Carson-Dellosa

RW: Underline Devon, package, ants, sandwich, mosquito, ear, cotton candy, Walter, socks, shoes, bag, dalmatians, fire engine, Sal, scissors, paper, Justin, lemons, lemonade, Polly, apple, Zoe, and music with yellow. Underline opened, crawled, buzzes, is, has, rode, used, squeezed, ate, and listened with blue.
DB: Answers will vary.

Page 49

Answers will vary.
RW: Underline Anna, grandmother, boots, phone, tissue, Ohio, dog, and pen with yellow. Underline held, shown, slept, and run with blue.
DB: Answers will vary.

Page 50

Answers will vary.

Page 51

Confusion — nouns, verbs, and adjectives

Nouns are words that name people, places, and things. Verbs are words that tell what someone or something is doing. Adjectives are words that describe nouns. Sometimes a word that is a noun in one sentence can be a verb or adjective in another sentence. How the word is used in a sentence determines what type of word it is.

example: That *fly* is bothering me. (noun)
example: I *fly* my kite. (verb)
example: Jamie caught the *fly* ball. (adjective)

What type of word is the underlined word in each sentence? Write adjective, noun, or verb on each line.

Sam will iron his *wrinkled* pants. ___adjective___
Jane *wrinkled* her nose at the nasty smell. ___verb___
The *ship* is docked at the pier. ___noun___
The Shoes Company will *ship* my new boots tomorrow. ___verb___
Goldfish live in a *liquid* environment. ___adjective___
This *liquid* will pour easily. ___noun___
Brad likes the *painted* horse best. ___adjective___
Fran *painted* her dresser blue. ___verb___
Vin *paints* many things. ___verb___
Katie bought a new set of *paints*. ___noun___

Review Work
Underline the verbs in the sentences with blue. Next to each sentence, write the verb tense: P = present, S = past, or F = future.

Draft Book
Think of two words that can be used as a noun and a verb. Write two sentences for each of the words. Use the words differently in each sentence.

© Carson-Dellosa   CD-4338 Grammar Rules! Grades 3–4   51

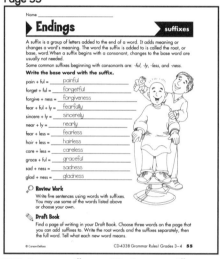

RW: Underline will iron, wrinkled, is docked, will ship, live, will pour, likes, painted, paints, and bought with blue. 1. F 2. S 3. P 4. F 5. P 6. F 7. P 8. S 9. P 10. S
DB: Answers will vary.

Page 52

Draw lines to match unhappy/not happy, bicycle/cycle with two wheels, rewind/wind again, uncover/not cover, uninformed/not informed, prewritten/written before, bimonthly/every two months, unknown/not known, and unicycle/cycle with one wheel. 1. not opened 2. washed before 3. every two weeks or two times a week
RW: Add uppercase letters and ending punctuation. DB: Answers will vary.

Page 53

At the End — suffixes -er and -est

A suffix is a group of letters added to the end of a word. It adds meaning or changes a word's meaning. The word the suffix is added to is called the root, or base, word. Most words just add endings; however, there are exceptions.
If a word ends with e, drop the e and add the ending: make - e + er = maker
If a word ends in y, change y to i and add the ending: happy - y + i + er = happier
If a word ends with a short vowel with one consonant, double the consonant and add the ending: fat + t + er = fatter
Two common suffixes are -er and -est. -Er means more. -Est means most. Sometimes when -er is added to a verb, however, it makes a noun that means someone who.
example: A painter is someone who paints.

Write the underlined base word with the correct ending.

The animal that is the most *mean* is the ___meanest___
The person who is the most *loud* is the ___loudest___
Someone who is more *fast* is the ___faster___
A person who *bakes* is a ___baker___
The child who is more *quiet* is the ___quieter___
A person who *swims* is a ___swimmer___
The person who is the most *angry* is the ___angriest___

Underline the word with a suffix. Write its meaning on the line.

your sunglasses are *darker* than mine ___more dark___
that is the *slowest* horse of the bunch ___most slow___
that aisle is *narrower* than it was before ___more narrow___

Review Work
Add uppercase letters and ending punctuation in the last three sentences.

Draft Book
Write ten sentences using words with the suffixes -er and -est.

© Carson-Dellosa   CD-4338 Grammar Rules! Grades 3–4   53

RW: Add uppercase letters and ending punctuation. DB: Answers will vary.

Page 54

Endings — suffixes

A suffix is a group of letters added to the end of a word. It adds meaning or changes a word's meaning. The word the suffix is added to is called the root, or base, word. When a suffix begins with a vowel, a change to the base word may be needed.
If a word ends with e, drop the e and add the ending: bake - e + ing = baking
If a word ends in a consonant + y, change y to i and add the ending (if adding -ing, keep the y and add -ing): carry - y + i + ed = carried   hurry + ing = hurrying
If a word ends in a vowel + y, add the ending: play + ing = playing
If a word has a short vowel with one consonant, double the consonant and add the ending: sun + n + y = sunny   bat + t + ed = batted
Some common suffixes that begin with vowels are: -ed, -ing, -able, -er, -y, and -est.

Write the base word with the suffix.

love + able = ___lovable___   bike + er = ___biker___
carry + ing = ___carrying___   nice + est = ___nicest___
stop + ed = ___stopped___   scurry + ed = ___scurried___
fun + y = ___funny___   identify + ing = ___identifying___

Circle the correct spelling.

Olive is (carriing / *carrying*) a large box.
Ian (multiplyed / *multiplied*) the two numbers.
Jerome is (rideing / *riding*) his bike.
Flora watched that (scarey / *scary*) movie.

Review Work
Underline the nouns in the sentences with yellow.

Draft Book
Make a list of words that use suffixes. Write the full word, then the suffix and base word separately. Use these words in future writing assignments.

54   CD-4338 Grammar Rules! Grades 3–4   © Carson-Dellosa

RW: Underline Olive, box, Ian, numbers, Jerome, bike, Flora, and movie with yellow.
DB: Answers will vary.

Page 55

Endings — suffixes

A suffix is a group of letters added to the end of a word. It adds meaning or changes a word's meaning. The word the suffix is added to is called the root, or base, word. When a suffix begins with a consonant, changes to the base word are usually not needed.
Some common suffixes beginning with consonants are: -ful, -ly, -less, and -ness.

Write the base word with the suffix.

pain + ful = ___painful___
forget + ful = ___forgetful___
forgive + ness = ___forgiveness___
fear + ful + ly = ___fearfully___
sincere + ly = ___sincerely___
near + ly = ___nearly___
fear + less = ___fearless___
hair + less = ___hairless___
care + less = ___careless___
grace + ful = ___graceful___
sad + ness = ___sadness___
glad + ness = ___gladness___

Review Work
Write five sentences using words with suffixes. You may use some of the words listed above or choose your own.

Draft Book
Find a page of writing in your Draft Book. Choose three words on the page that you can add suffixes to. Write the root words and the suffixes separately, then the full word. Tell what each new word means.

© Carson-Dellosa   CD-4338 Grammar Rules! Grades 3–4   55

RW: Answers will vary. DB: Answers will vary.

Page 56

How, Where, or When — adverbs

Adverbs are words that tell more about verbs. They tell how, where, or when something happens.

Underline the verb in each sentence. Circle the adverbs that tell how, where, and when.

Janice *closes* the book (quickly).
Tito (frequently) *plays* in the park.
Missie *will watch* that movie (tonight).
Zack *worked* (quietly) on his model.
Leo *ran* on the bike path (last week).
Pete and Susie *flew* to their grandma's (yesterday).
Walter *will miss* his game (tomorrow).
Tracy *mixed* the ingredients (carefully).
Rick *will eat* strawberries (later).
Ariel (often) *stops* to pick flowers.

Review Work
Underline the nouns in the sentences with yellow.

Draft Book
Write a story about your favorite movie. Include adverbs. Circle the adverbs with purple.

56   CD-4338 Grammar Rules! Grades 3–4   © Carson-Dellosa

RW: Underline Janice, book, Tito, park, Missie, movie, Zack, model, Leo, path, Pete, Susie, grandma's, Walter, game, Tracy, ingredients, Rick, strawberries, Ariel, and flowers with yellow. DB: Answers will vary.

How Was It Done? `adverbs`

Adverbs are words that tell more about verbs. They tell how, where, or when something happens.

What does each adverb tell about the verb? Write how, where, or when on each line. Draw an arrow to the verb the adverb is telling more about.

Kylie worked **smarter** than she had in the past. _____ how

Neil swam **through** the channel. _____ where

Archie jogs **daily**. _____ when

The wind **wildly** blew the branches. _____ how

Rico complained **loudly**. _____ how

The storm will be here **soon**. _____ where

Jennifer **never** cheats. _____ when

Jade **cheerfully** sets the table. _____ when

Ian **always** wears his bike helmet. _____ when

Simon rubbed the wet dog **vigorously** with a towel. _____ how

After playing all day, Gwen went **inside** to relax. _____ how

Meg put the cookies **up** on the shelf. _____ where

Review Work
Underline the nouns in the sentences with yellow.

Draft Book
Write a story about a thunderstorm you remember. Include adverbs. Circle the adverbs with purple.

© Carson-Dellosa — CD-4338 Grammar Rules! Grades 3–4 **57**

RW: Underline Kylie, past, Neil, channel, Archie, wind, branches, Rico, storm, Jennifer, Jade, table, Ian, helmet, Simon, dog, towel, day, Gwen, Meg, cookies, and shelf with yellow. DB: Answers will vary.

Page 58: Answers will vary.

Page 59

Mathematics `articles a, an, the`

A, an, and the are articles. An article comes before a noun or adjective/noun combination. Use a in front of words that start with a consonant sound. Use an in front of words that start with a vowel sound. Use the if reference is being made to a specific thing or things.

Write a or an in front of these mathematical items.

an	intersection	a	cone
an	addend	a	multiple
a	right triangle	an	addition problem
a	fraction	a	subtraction symbol
an	equal sign	a	sum
a	difference	an	even number
an	ordered pair	an	odd number

Write a, an, or the on the lines.

Lillie is learning about shapes in math. She draws ___an___ oval on her paper. ___An___ oval has no corners or sides. Next, she draws ___an___ octagon, which is ___an___ eight-sided figure. Then, Lillie draws ___a___ figure with ___an___ acute angle. Lillie enjoys drawing ___the___ different shapes. Now, she will color ___the___ shapes with ___a___ marker.

Review Work
Circle the uppercase letter at the beginning of each sentence and the ending punctuation.

Draft Book
Find a story you have written in your Draft Book. Circle the articles in orange. If an article is incorrect, fix it.

© Carson-Dellosa — CD-4338 Grammar Rules! Grades 3–4 **59**

RW: Circle beginning uppercase letters and ending punctuation. DB: Answers will vary.

Page 60

Pick the Pronoun `subject pronouns`

A pronoun takes the place of a noun. Subject pronouns take the place of the simple subject nouns. They are: I, you, he, she, we, they, and it.

Above each group of words, write the pronoun that could replace each word in the group. Add four nouns to each list.

it
helicopter
antelope
statue
computer

she
my sister
Ms. Lee
Betsy
Grandma

they
the kindergartners
Pete, Jan, and Leon
the crowd
that family

we
my class and I
my sister and I
my team and I
you and I

he
Dad
my brother
Mr. Nelson
Ned

Review Work
Draw an X next to each proper noun.

Draft Book
Write a story about your friends. Underline the subject pronouns with red.

60 CD-4338 Grammar Rules! Grades 3–4 — © Carson-Dellosa

Page 60 (cont.)
Lists will vary.
RW: Draw an X next to Ms. Lee, Betsy, Grandma, Pete, Jan, Leon, Dad, Mr. Nelson, and Ned. DB: Answers will vary.

Page 61

Who Did It? `subject pronouns`

A pronoun takes the place of a noun. A subject pronoun usually comes before a verb. Subject pronouns take the place of the simple subject nouns. They are: I, you, he, she, we, they, and it.

Replace each noun in bold type with a subject pronoun. Write the correct pronoun on the line.

Dillon's **sheep** produced bags of wool. _____ It

Alexis and Anika live in Hong Kong. _____ They

Mr. Arc is my math teacher. _____ He

Jeremy dove into the pool. _____ He

My bike needs a new tire. _____ It

Mary won first prize. _____ She

The sun toasted my nose. _____ It

Judy caught an enormous fish. _____ She

Anna and I made a castle at the beach. _____ We

Write two sentences using the pronoun you.

_____

_____

Write two sentences using the pronoun I.

_____

_____

Review Work
Underline the nouns in the sentences with yellow.

Draft Book
Find a page of writing in your Draft Book. Change the subject nouns to subject pronouns.

© Carson-Dellosa — CD-4338 Grammar Rules! Grades 3–4 **61**

Sentences will vary.
RW: Underline sheep, bags, wool, Alexis, Anika, Hong Kong, Mr. Arc, teacher, Jeremy, pool, bike, tire, Mary, prize, sun, nose, Judy, fish, Anna, castle, and beach with yellow. DB: Answers will vary.

Page 62

Past the Verb `object pronouns`

An object pronoun takes the place of a noun found in the complete predicate. An object pronoun usually comes after a verb. Object pronouns are: me, you, her, him, them, us, and it.

Replace each noun in bold type with an object pronoun. Write the correct pronoun on the line.

Fiona lobbed the **tennis ball** to Sarah. _____ it

Gena and I told the secret to **David**. _____ him

Dillon sent the package to **Blake and Hailey**. _____ them

Mrs. Mars read the book with **Willie and me**. _____ us

Spencer spoke on the phone with **Dan**. _____ him

The basketball swished through the **hoop**. _____ it

Sydney biked to the park with **Jessica**. _____ her

Lars handed the **salt** to Timothy. _____ it

The garbage truck knocked the **garbage cans** over. _____ them

Alexis made a sand castle with **Reanne and me**. _____ us

Write a sentence using the object pronoun me and one with the object pronoun you. Remember to place each pronoun after the verb.
example: The bright sun gave me a headache.

_____

_____

Review Work
Underline the nouns with yellow. Write the correct subject pronouns above the nouns that are before the verbs.

Draft Book
Write a story about a book you read recently. Use subject and object pronouns in your story. Underline the pronouns with red.

62 CD-4338 Grammar Rules! Grades 3–4 — © Carson-Dellosa

Sentences will vary.
RW: Underline Fiona, ball, Sarah, Gena, secret, David, Dillon, package, Blake, Hailey, Mrs. Mars, book, Willie, Spencer, phone, Dan, basketball, hoop, Sydney, park, Jessica, Lars, salt, Timothy, truck, cans, Alexis, sand castle, and Reanne with yellow. 1. She 2. She 3. He/She 4. She 5. He 6. It 7. She 8. He 9. It 10. She DB: Answers will vary.

Page 63

I or Me? `pronouns`

Pronouns take the place of nouns. Subject pronouns take the place of subject nouns. Object pronouns take the place of predicate nouns. A subject pronoun usually comes before a verb. An object pronoun usually comes after a verb. subject pronouns: I, you, he, she, we, they, it; object pronouns: me, you, her, him, them, us, it.

Circle the correct pronoun.

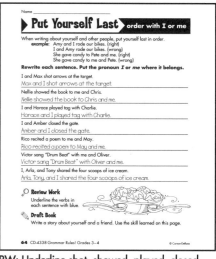

(I), Me) went to the library.

Can you come to the pool with (we, (us))?

(He), Him) helped (I, (me)) put up the poster.

Hannah delivered the package to (they, (them)).

(She), Her) caught a butterfly.

(We), Us) will build a tree fort.

Did ((he), him) get a turn?

Joe threw the ball to ((he), (him)).

Karen likes soccer, but ((she), her) likes golf better.

Mr. Paulson checked out the book to (she, (her)).

((She), Her) will put the stamp on the envelope. Then, ((she), her) will mail it.

(We), Us) went with (she, (her)) to the store.

Review Work
Draw an X next to each proper noun.

Draft Book
Find a page of writing in your Draft Book. Underline the pronouns with red. Make corrections where necessary.

© Carson-Dellosa — CD-4338 Grammar Rules! Grades 3–4 **63**

RW: Draw an X next to Hannah, Joe, Karen, and Mr. Paulson. DB: Answers will vary.

Page 64

Put Yourself Last `order with I or me`

When writing about yourself and other people, put yourself last in order.
example: Amy and I rode our bikes. (right)
I and Amy rode our bikes. (wrong)
She gave candy to Pete and me. (right)
She gave candy to me and Pete. (wrong)

Rewrite each sentence. Put the pronoun I or me where it belongs.

I and Max shot arrows at the target.
Max and I shot arrows at the target.

Nellie showed the book to me and Chris.
Nellie showed the book to Chris and me.

I and Horace played tag with Charlie.
Horace and I played tag with Charlie.

I and Amber closed the gate.
Amber and I closed the gate.

Rico recited a poem to me and May.
Rico recited a poem to May and me.

Victor sang "Drum Beat" with me and Oliver.
Victor sang "Drum Beat" with Oliver and me.

I, Arla, and Tony shared the four scoops of ice cream.
Arla, Tony, and I shared the four scoops of ice cream.

Review Work
Underline the verbs in each sentence with blue.

Draft Book
Write a story about yourself and a friend. Use the skill learned on this page.

64 CD-4338 Grammar Rules! Grades 3–4 — © Carson-Dellosa

RW: Underline shot, showed, played, closed, recited, sang, and shared with blue. DB: Answers will vary.

Page 65

My Bike Bumped His Bike `possessive pronouns`

Possessive pronouns take the place of possessive nouns. They are: my, your, his, her, its, our, and their. The possessive pronoun its does not have an apostrophe.

Write the correct possessive pronoun on each line.

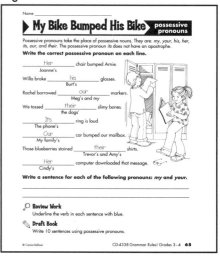

_____ Her _____ chair bumped Arnie.
Joanne's

Willa broke _____ his _____ glasses.
Burt's

Rachel borrowed _____ our _____ markers.
Meg's and my

We tossed _____ their _____ slimy bones.
the dogs'

_____ Its _____ ring is loud.
The phone's

_____ Our _____ car bumped our mailbox.
My family's

Those blueberries stained _____ their _____ shirts.
Trevor's and Amy's

_____ Her _____ computer downloaded that message.
Cindy's

Write a sentence for each of the following pronouns: my and your.

_____

_____

Review Work
Underline the verb in each sentence with blue.

Draft Book
Write 10 sentences using possessive pronouns.

© Carson-Dellosa — CD-4338 Grammar Rules! Grades 3–4 **65**

© Carson-Dellosa

Page 65 (cont.)
Sentences will vary.
RW: Underline bumped, broke, borrowed, tossed, is, bumped, stained, and downloaded with blue. DB: Answers will vary.

Page 66

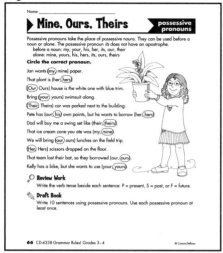

Name _____

▶ Mine, Ours, Theirs — possessive pronouns

Possessive pronouns take the place of possessive nouns. They can be used before a noun or alone. The possessive pronoun *its* does not have an apostrophe.
before a noun: my, your, his, her, its, our, their
alone: mine, yours, his, hers, its, ours, theirs

Circle the correct pronoun.
Jan wants (my, mine) paper.
That plant is (her, hers).
(Our, Ours) house is the white one with blue trim.
Bring (your, yours) swimsuit along.
(Their, Theirs) car was parked next to the building.
Pete has (our, his) own paints, but he wants to borrow (her, hers).
Dad will buy me a swing set like (their, theirs).
That ice cream cone you ate was (my, mine).
We will bring (our, ours) lunches on the field trip.
(Her, Hers) scissors dropped on the floor.
That team lost their bat, so they borrowed (our, ours).
Kelly has a bike, but she wants to use (your, yours).

🔎 **Review Work**
Write the verb tense beside each sentence: P = present, S = past, or F = future.

✏️ **Draft Book**
Write 10 sentences using possessive pronouns. Use each possessive pronoun at least once.

66 CD-4338 Grammar Rules! Grades 3-4   © Carson-Dellosa

RW: 1. P 2. P 3. P 4. P 5. S 6. P 7. F 8. S 9. F 10. S 11. S 12. P DB: Answers will vary.

Page 67

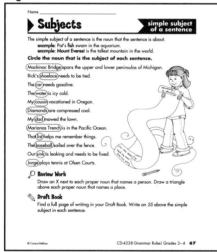

Name _____

▶ Subjects — simple subject of a sentence

The simple subject of a sentence is the noun that the sentence is about.
example: Pat's fish swam in the aquarium.
example: Mount Everest is the tallest mountain in the world.

Circle the noun that is the subject of each sentence.
(Mackinac Bridge) spans the upper and lower peninsulas of Michigan.
Rick's (shoelace) needs to be tied.
The (car) needs gasoline.
The (water) is icy cold.
My (cousin) vacationed in Oregon.
(Diamonds) are compressed coal.
My (dad) mowed the lawn.
(Marianas Trench) is in the Pacific Ocean.
That (list) helps me remember things.
The (baseball) sailed over the fence.
Our (sink) is leaking and needs to be fixed.
(Jorge) plays tennis at Olsen Courts.

🔎 **Review Work**
Draw an X next to each proper noun that names a person. Draw a triangle above each proper noun that names a place.

✏️ **Draft Book**
Find a full page of writing in your Draft Book. Write an *SS* above the simple subject in each sentence.

© Carson-Dellosa   CD-4338 Grammar Rules! Grades 3-4 67

RW: Draw an X next to Rick and Jorge. Draw a triangle above Mackinac Bridge, Michigan, Oregon, Marianas Trench, Pacific Ocean, and Olsen Courts. DB: Answers will vary.

Page 68
Answers will vary.
RW: Underline people, dates, trees, sky, fruit, water, and game with yellow.
DB: Answers will vary.

Page 69

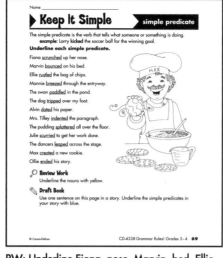

Name _____

▶ Keep It Simple — simple predicate

The simple predicate is the verb that tells what someone or something is doing.
example: Larry kicked the soccer ball for the winning goal.

Underline each simple predicate.
Fiona scrunched up her nose.
Marvin bounced on his bed.
Ellie rustled the bag of chips.
Mannie breezed through the entryway.
The swan paddled in the pond.
The dog tripped over my foot.
Alvin dated his paper.
Mrs. Tilley indented the paragraph.
The pudding splattered all over the floor.
Julie scurried to get her work done.
The dancers leaped across the stage.
Max created a new cookie.
Ollie ended his story.

🔎 **Review Work**
Underline the nouns with yellow.

✏️ **Draft Book**
Use one sentence on this page in a story. Underline the simple predicates in your story with blue.

© Carson-Dellosa   CD-4338 Grammar Rules! Grades 3-4 69

RW: Underline Fiona, nose, Marvin, bed, Ellie, bag, chips, Mannie, entryway, swan, pond, dog, foot, Alvin, paper, Mrs. Tilley, paragraph, pudding, floor, Julie, work, dancers, stage, Max, cookie, Ollie, and story with yellow.
DB: Answers will vary.

Page 70

Name _____

▶ Entomology — simple subjects and predicates

The simple predicate is the verb that tells what someone or something is doing.
Underline each simple subject once. Underline the simple predicate twice.

Bees buzz.   A hornet stings.
A grasshopper hops.   Ants scurry.
Butterflies migrate.   Silkworms spin.
A caterpillar crawls.   Ladybugs swarm.
A dragonfly hovers.   A cicada hums.

Write the singular nouns with their verbs here.
grasshopper hops   hornet stings
caterpillar crawls   cicada hums
dragonfly hovers

Write the plural nouns with their verbs here.
bees buzz   silkworms spin
butterflies migrate   ladybugs swarm
ants scurry

🔎 **Review Work**
Choose a sentence with a singular noun. Rewrite it to make the noun plural.

✏️ **Draft Book**
Find a page of writing in your Draft Book. Choose five sentences from that page and rewrite them. If a noun is singular, make it plural. If a noun is plural, make it singular. Remember to change each verb, too!

70 CD-4338 Grammar Rules! Grades 3-4   © Carson-Dellosa

RW: Answers will vary. DB: Answers will vary.

Page 71

Name _____

▶ The Whole Thing — complete subject

The simple subject is the noun that the sentence is about. The complete subject is the simple subject plus any articles or adjectives that describe or modify that noun.
example: The striped ball rolled down the hill.
ball = simple subject
The striped ball = complete subject
article   adjective

Circle the simple subject. Underline the complete subject.
My third-grade (teacher) wrote on the overhead projector.
The little, purple (candy) tingles on my tongue.
That enormous (elephant) trumpeted for an hour.
The glowing, hot (lava) poured down the hillside.
That skinny, black (pen) writes perfectly.
The noisy, bright, exciting (carnival) will close at 9:00.
(Anna Rice) will throw the ball.
Her new (watch) broke yesterday.
The large, fierce (lion) cowered in the corner.
The sticky (glue) spilled onto Brin's pants.

🔎 **Review Work**
Underline the simple predicates with blue. Write the verb tense beside each sentence: P = present, S = past, and F = future.

✏️ **Draft Book**
Write 10 sentences with articles or adjectives modifying the simple subjects. Circle the simple subjects and underline the complete subjects.

© Carson-Dellosa   CD-4338 Grammar Rules! Grades 3-4 71

Page 71 (cont.)
RW: Underline wrote, tingles, trumpeted, poured, writes, close, throw, broke, cowered, and spilled with blue. 1. S 2. P 3. S 4. S 5. P 6. F 7. F 8. S 9. S 10. S
DB: Answers will vary.

Page 72

Name _____

▶ Completeness — complete subject

The simple subject is the noun that the sentence is about. The complete subject is the simple subject plus any articles or adjectives that describe or modify that noun.
example: The tall oak tree swayed in the breeze.
tree = simple subject
The tall oak tree = complete subject
article   adjectives
Sometimes the simple subject is the complete subject.
example: Don ran home.
Don is the simple subject. Don is also the complete subject.

Circle the simple subject. Underline the complete subject.
(Blaine) weeded the garden.
(Erika) toured the village.
Winnie's little golden (guinea pig) ran under the dresser.
The overdone (hamburgers) tasted bad.
(Horns) blared on the street.
The recess (bell) rang.
(Tim) will make his bed.
An oxygen (tank) assists deep-sea divers.
Prickly (cactus) survive in hot deserts.
My (ring) fell into the sink.

🔎 **Review Work**
Underline the simple predicates with blue. Write the verb tense beside each sentence: P = present, S = past, and F = future.

✏️ **Draft Book**
Write 10 sentences with articles or adjectives modifying the simple subjects. Circle the simple subjects and underline the complete subjects.

72 CD-4338 Grammar Rules! Grades 3-4   © Carson-Dellosa

RW: Underline weeded, toured, ran, tasted, blared, rang, make, assists, survive, and fell with blue. 1. S 2. S 3. S 4. S 5. S 6. S 7. F 8. P 9. P 10. S DB: Answers will vary.

Page 73

Name _____

▶ That One — complete subject

The complete subject is the simple subject plus any articles or adjectives that describe or modify that noun. It can also include other modifiers you have not yet learned to identify.
example: The (cup) of hot chocolate is empty.
The (monkey) by the feeding bowl threw a banana.
The (apple) with a bruise fell on the floor.

Circle the simple subject. Underline the complete subject.
That (puppy) by the bench dug this big hole.
The snorkeling (group) of 15 swam near the reef.
(Flowers) from that garden smell wonderful.
The (canoe) alongside the dock took me to the island.
The (parrot) with a green head will belong to Ned when he pays for it.
The brown (horse) brushed my shoulder with her nose.
The slimy (earthworms) in that pile of leaves are great fish bait.
The moldy (bread) in the garbage looks awful.
(Frogs) will swim in this pond when it's warmer.
That (candle) on the table burns brightly.

🔎 **Review Work**
Underline the simple predicates with blue. Write the verb tense beside each sentence: P = present, S = past, and F = future.

✏️ **Draft Book**
Write 10 sentences. Circle the simple subjects and underline the complete subjects.

© Carson-Dellosa   CD-4338 Grammar Rules! Grades 3-4 73

RW: Underline dug, swam, smell, took, belong, brushed, are, looks, swim, and burns with blue. 1. S 2. S 3. P 4. S 5. F 6. S 7. P 8. P 9. F 10. P
DB: Answers will vary.

CD-4338 Grammar Rules! Grades 3-4 **123**

Here We Go — complete predicate

The simple predicate is the verb that tells what someone or something is doing. The complete predicate is the simple predicate plus any helping or linking verbs and any adverbs that describe or modify the verb.

example: The ball will roll smoothly.
roll = simple predicate
will roll smoothly = complete predicate
helping verb *adverb*

Circle the simple predicate. Underline the complete predicate twice.

Jake often reads quickly.
The snow frequently fell rapidly.
The rain pounded loudly last night.
The wet dog shook vigorously.
An ant may have wandered around yesterday.
June never screams loudly.
That koala will eat constantly.
That lion could lunge immediately.
Lena may finish tonight.
Those tennis shoes smell awful.

Review Work
Identify the verb tense of each sentence. Write the verb tense beside each sentence: P = present, S = past, and F = future.

Draft Book
Write 10 sentences with helping or linking verbs and adverbs modifying the simple predicates. Circle the simple predicates and underline the complete predicates twice.

74 CD-4338 Grammar Rules! Grades 3–4 © Carson-Dellosa

RW: 1. P 2. S 3. S 4. S 5. S 6. P 7. F 8. F 9. F 10. P DB: Answers will vary.

Page 75

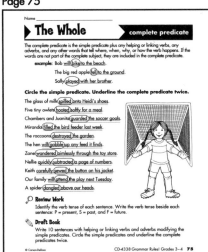

The Whole — complete predicate

The complete predicate is the simple predicate plus any helping verbs, any adverbs, and any other words that tell where, when, why, or how the verb happens. If the words are not part of the complete subject, they are included in the complete predicate.

example: Bob will bike to the beach.
The big red apple fell to the ground.
Sally played with her brother.

Circle the simple predicate. Underline the complete predicate twice.

The glass of milk spilled onto Heidi's shoes.
Five tiny owlets hooted softly for a meal.
Chambers and Juanita guarded the soccer goals.
Miranda filled the bird feeder last week.
The raccoons destroyed the garden.
The hen will gobble up any feed it finds.
Zane wandered aimlessly through the toy store.
Nellie quickly subtracted a page of numbers.
Keith carefully sewed the button on his jacket.
Our family will attend the play next Tuesday.
A spider dangled above our heads.

Review Work
Identify the verb tense of each sentence. Write the verb tense beside each sentence: P = present, S = past, and F = future.

Draft Book
Write 10 sentences with helping or linking verbs and adverbs modifying the predicates. Circle the simple predicates and underline the complete predicates twice.

© Carson-Dellosa CD-4338 Grammar Rules! Grades 3–4 75

RW: 1. S 2. S 3. S 4. S 5. S 6. F 7. S 8. S 9. S 10. F 11. S DB: Answers will vary.

Page 76

Do Tell — complete subjects and predicates

The complete subject tells who or what the sentence is about. The complete predicate tells what the someone or something is doing.

Underline the complete subject once. Underline the complete predicate twice.

The noisy movie prevented Kris from working.
The box of tissues emptied quickly.
The old, rusty swing continues to be the kids' favorite.
Pete loads the back of the truck with plants.
Many shiny marbles scattered across the tile floor.
Many important men signed the Declaration of Independence.
Few tomato plants survived the dog's digging.
The steep cliff towered above the river.
The remote-controlled car raced along the sidewalk.
The giant toad devoured many insects.
The tape secured the picture to the wall.

Review Work
Write an SS above the simple subject in each sentence. Circle the simple predicates.

Draft Book
Locate a page of writing in your Draft Book. Underline each complete subject once. Underline each complete predicate twice.

76 CD-4338 Grammar Rules! Grades 3–4 © Carson-Dellosa

Page 76 (cont.)

RW: Write an SS above movie, box, swing, Pete, marbles, men, plants, cliff, car, toad, and tape. Circle prevented, emptied, continues, loads, scattered, signed, survived, towered, raced, devoured, and secured.
DB: Answers will vary.

Page 77

Star or X — complete sentences

A sentence needs one complete subject and one complete predicate to be a sentence.

example: Jan has a dog. = sentence
complete subject   complete predicate
a dog ≠ not a sentence

A sentence can be long or short.
example: Jan walks.
complete subject   complete predicate
example: The tiny little bird with the broken wing → complete subject
finally flew out the door and into the backyard. ← complete predicate

If the group of words is a sentence, put a star in the box. Underline the complete subject once. Underline the complete predicate twice. If the group of words is not a sentence, put an X in the box.

X	The old yellow lion in the cage.	☆	Carrots are healthy.
X	Walking through the quiet hallway.	☆	That butterfly is beautiful.
X	Many little.	☆	Jake closed it.
☆	The strawberries are tasty.	☆	Josie walks to school.
X	Are very large.	X	Going here?
X	In that really scary house.	X	The woods are.
☆	Camp is fun.	X	This bubble gum.

Review Work
Write the linking verbs used in the groups of words from above.
are, is

Draft Book
Make complete sentences using each group of words that has an X in the box.

© Carson-Dellosa CD-4338 Grammar Rules! Grades 3–4 77

DB: Answers will vary.

Page 78: Answers will vary.

Page 79

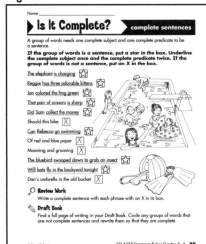

Is It Complete? — complete sentences

A group of words needs one complete subject and one complete predicate to be a sentence.

If the group of words is a sentence, put a star in the box. Underline the complete subject once and the complete predicate twice. If the group of words is not a sentence, put an X in the box.

The elephant is charging ☆
Reggie has three adorable kittens ☆
Jon colored the frog green ☆
That pair of scissors is sharp ☆
Did Sam collect the money ☆
Should his bike X
Can Rebecca go swimming ☆
Of red and blue paper X
Moaning and groaning X
The bluebird swooped down to grab an insect ☆
Will bats fly in the backyard tonight ☆
Dan's umbrella in the old bucket X

Review Work
Write a complete sentence with each phrase with an X in its box.

Draft Book
Find a full page of writing in your Draft Book. Circle any groups of words that are not complete sentences and rewrite them so that they are complete.

© Carson-Dellosa CD-4338 Grammar Rules! Grades 3–4 79

RW: Answers will vary. DB: Answers will vary.

Page 80

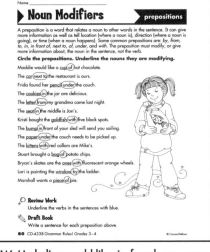

Noun Modifiers — prepositions

A preposition is a word that relates a noun to other words in the sentence. It can give more information as well as tell location (where a noun is), direction (where a noun is going), or time (when a noun happens). Some common prepositions are: by, from, to, in, in front of, next to, of, under, and with. The preposition must modify, or give more information about, the noun in the sentence, not the verb.

Circle the prepositions. Underline the nouns they are modifying.

Maddie would like a cup of hot chocolate.
The car next to the restaurant is ours.
Frida found her pencil under the couch.
The cookies in the jar are delicious.
The letter from my grandma came last night.
The seat in the middle is Jon's.
Kristi bought the goldfish with five black spots.
The bump in front of your sled will send you sailing.
The paper under the couch needs to be picked up.
The kittens with red collars are Mike's.
Stuart brought a bag of potato chips.
Bryan's skates are the ones with fluorescent orange wheels.
Lori is painting the window by the ladder.
Marshall wants a piece of pie.

Review Work
Underline the verbs in the sentences with blue.

Draft Book
Write a sentence for each preposition above.

80 CD-4338 Grammar Rules! Grades 3–4 © Carson-Dellosa

RW: Underline would like, is, found, are, came, is, bought, will send, needs, are, brought, are, is painting, and wants with blue.
DB: Answers will vary.

Page 81

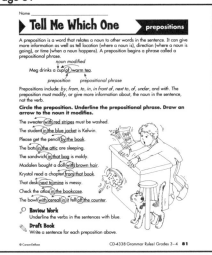

Tell Me Which One — prepositions

A preposition is a word that relates a noun to other words in the sentence. It can give more information as well as tell location (where a noun is), direction (where a noun is going), or time (when a noun happens). A preposition begins a phrase called a prepositional phrase.

noun modified
Meg drinks a cup of warm tea.
preposition   prepositional phrase

Prepositions include: by, from, to, in, in front of, next to, of, under, and with. The preposition must modify, or give more information about, the noun in the sentence, not the verb.

Circle the preposition. Underline the prepositional phrase. Draw an arrow to the noun it modifies.

The sweater with red stripes must be washed.
The student in the blue jacket is Kelvin.
Please get the pencil by the book.
The bats in the attic are sleeping.
The sandwich in that bag is moldy.
Madelen bought a doll with brown hair.
Krystal read a chapter from that book.
That desk next to mine is messy.
Check the atlas in the bookcase.
The bowl with cereal in it fell off the counter.

Review Work
Underline the verbs in the sentences with blue.

Draft Book
Write a sentence for each preposition above.

© Carson-Dellosa CD-4338 Grammar Rules! Grades 3–4 81

RW: Underline must be washed, is, get, are sleeping, is, bought, read, is, check, and fell with blue. DB: Answers will vary.

Page 82

We Sound the Same — homophones

Homophones are words that sound alike but are spelled differently and have different meanings.

Write the correct homophone on the line.

threw: verb, past tense of throw   through: between, from one side to another
Victoria walked _through_ the door.
Paulina looked _through_ the window.
Angelica _threw_ the winning pass.

sent: verb, past tense of send   scent: a smell   cent: unit of money
The _scent_ of that flower is faint.
Mr. Hill _sent_ Allison to the office.
This penny is worth one _cent_.

its: possessive pronoun   it's: contraction for it is
_It's_ very hot outside.
The class has _its_ own drinking fountain.
Brinley thinks _it's_ too cold to go in the pool.
Its place is on that shelf.

whole: entire   hole: part missing
The _whole_ class is going on a field trip.
Jeremiah wanted the _whole_ apple.
There is a _hole_ in this sock.

Review Work
Underline the nouns with yellow.

Draft Book
Choose one pair of homophones. Write two sentences with each word.

82 CD-4338 Grammar Rules! Grades 3–4 © Carson-Dellosa

© Carson-Dellosa

Page 82 (cont.)
RW: Underline Victoria, door, Paulina, window, Angelica, pass, flower, Mr. Hill, Allison, office, cent, penny, outside, class, fountain, Brinley, pool, place, shelf, class, field trip, Jeremiah, apple, hole, and sock with yellow.
DB: Answers will vary.

Page 83

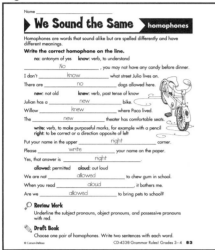

> Name _____
>
> ### ▶ We Sound the Same   homophones
>
> Homophones are words that sound alike but are spelled differently and have different meanings.
> **Write the correct homophone on the line.**
> na: antonym of yes   know: verb, to understand
> I don't _____No_____ , you may not have any candy before dinner.
> There are _____no_____ what street Julio lives on.
> _____ dogs allowed here.
>
> new: not old   knew: verb, past tense of know
> Julian has a _____new_____ bike.
> Willow _____knew_____ where Paco lived.
> The _____new_____ theater has comfortable seats.
>
> write: verb, to make purposeful marks, for example with a pencil
> right: to be correct or a direction opposite of left
> Put your name in the upper _____right_____ corner.
> Please _____write_____ your name on the paper.
> Yes, that answer is _____right_____ .
>
> allowed: permitted   aloud: out loud
> We are not _____allowed_____ to chew gum in school.
> When you read _____aloud_____ , it bothers me.
> Are we _____allowed_____ to bring pets to school?
>
> ○ **Review Work**
> Underline the subject pronouns, object pronouns, and possessive pronouns with red.
>
> ✎ **Draft Book**
> Choose one pair of homophones. Write two sentences with each word.
>
> © Carson-Dellosa   CD-4338 Grammar Rules! Grades 3–4   **83**

RW: Underline you, I, your, your, we, you, it, me, and we with red.
DB: Answers will vary.

Page 84

> Name _____
>
> ### ▶ We Sound the Same   homophones
>
> Homophones are words that sound alike but are spelled differently and have different meanings.
> **Write the correct homophone on the line.**
> here: location word   hear: to understand sound by way of the ear
> Did you _____hear_____ the owl hooting last night?
> They were _____here_____ last night.
> You can sit _____here_____ beside me.
> Sorry, I couldn't _____hear_____ you.
>
> by: near   buy: to purchase
> Put the pencil _____by_____ the stack of books.
> I would like to _____buy_____ that toy.
> Where can I _____buy_____ new shoes?
> Kelly is standing _____by_____ the water fountain.
>
> there: location word   their: possessive pronoun   they're: contraction for they are
> Would you put this paper over _____there_____ ?
> He will go _____there_____ for vacation.
> Do you think _____their_____ mother likes snakes?
> _____They're_____ bringing a snake home.
> I think _____they're_____ still in gym.
>
> ○ **Review Work**
> Underline the subject pronouns, object pronouns, and possessive pronouns with red.
>
> ✎ **Draft Book**
> Choose one pair of homophones. Write two sentences with each word.
>
> **84** CD-4338 Grammar Rules! Grades 3–4   © Carson-Dellosa

RW: Underline you, they, you, me, I, you, I, I, you, he, you, they, I, and they with red.
DB: Answers will vary.

Page 85

> Name _____
>
> ### ▶ To, Too, Two   homophones
>
> To, too, and two are homophones.
> **to** is used in place of toward or with a verb: Rita went to school.
>   I like to eat candy.
> **two** is a number word for the numeral 2: Ian has two sisters.
> **too** means also or more than enough: Zane wants some milk, too.
>   That music is too noisy.
>
> **Write to, too, or two on each line.**
> talia left at _____two_____ o'clock
> is that soup _____too_____ hot
> are you tired, _____too_____
> _____Two_____ lions roared
> my aunt plans _____to_____ come _____to_____ our soccer game, _____too_____
> you can have _____two_____ stickers, _____too_____
> toni went _____to_____ _____two_____ amusement parks this summer
> anthony broke _____two_____ crayons
> we saw _____two_____ hours of fireworks
> angelica threw the ball _____to_____ aaron
> please give those _____two_____ crickets _____to_____ george
> sheila will mail the letter _____to_____ olicia
>
> ○ **Review Work**
> Add uppercase letters and ending punctuation.
>
> ✎ **Draft Book**
> Write three sentences with each meaning of these homophones.
>
> CD-4338 Grammar Rules! Grades 3–4   **85**

RW: Add uppercase letters and ending punctuation. DB: Answers will vary.

Page 86

> Name _____
>
> ### ▶ Evening   declarative sentences
>
> A declarative sentence tells something. It begins with an uppercase letter and ends with a period.
> **Cross out the first letter of each sentence and write the uppercase letter next to it. Put a period at the end of each sentence.**
>
> T̶he sky is beginning to darken
> A̶ shooting star streaked across the sky
> I̶ wonder how far away the nearest star is
> H̶aley looked at stars through the telescope
> L̶ourdes saw Jupiter and Venus last night
> T̶he stars are not as bright as the moon
> M̶any noises can be heard at night
> I̶ don't like night noises that are scary
> T̶he full moon is rising above the trees
> I̶ heard an owl hoot
> I̶t is time to go to bed
>
> ○ **Review Work**
> Circle the adjectives with orange.
>
> ✎ **Draft Book**
> Write six interrogative and six declarative sentences. Begin each sentence with an uppercase letter and end it with the correct punctuation mark.
>
> **86** CD-4338 Grammar Rules! Grades 3–4   © Carson-Dellosa

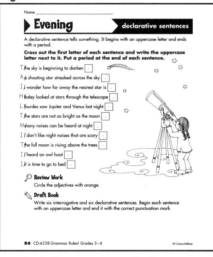

RW: Circle shooting, nearest, bright, many, night, scary, and full with orange.
DB: Answers will vary.

Page 87

> Name _____
>
> ### ▶ I Want to Know   interrogative sentences
>
> An interrogative sentence asks a question. It begins with an uppercase letter and ends with a question mark.
> **Rewrite each interrogative sentence. Put an uppercase letter at the beginning and a question mark at the end.**
>
> who owns that red bike
> Who owns that red bike?
> what kind of insect is that
> What kind of insect is that?
> how did the kite get stuck in that tree
> How did the kite get stuck in that tree?
> where do fruit bats sleep
> Where do fruit bats sleep?
> who gave the Statue of Liberty to the United States
> Who gave the Statue of Liberty to the United States?
> do tarantulas live in Arkansas
> Do tarantulas live in Arkansas?
> will you turn off that loud music
> Will you turn off that loud music?
> are those cookies still hot
> Are those cookies still hot?
>
> ○ **Review Work**
> Some of the sentences above have linking or helping verbs. Underline these verbs with blue.
>
> ✎ **Draft Book**
> Write five interrogative sentences. Begin each sentence with an uppercase letter and end it with a question mark.
>
> CD-4338 Grammar Rules! Grades 3–4   **87**

Page 87 (cont.)
RW: Underline is, did, do, do, will, and are with blue. DB: Answers will vary.

Page 88

> Name _____
>
> ### ▶ Where?   declarative and interrogative sentences
>
> A declarative sentence tells something and ends with a period. An interrogative sentence asks a question and ends with a question mark.
> **Put the correct punctuation mark at the end of each sentence. Answer the question with a declarative sentence using the information given.**
>
> Kangaroos live where koalas live [.] Koalas live in Australia [.]
> Where do kangaroos live [?]
> Kangaroos live in Australia.
> Wild penguins do not live north of the equator [.] Alaska is north of the equator [.]
> Do wild penguins live in Alaska [?]
> Wild penguins do not live in Alaska.
> Monarch butterflies migrate to Michigan in the spring [.] These butterflies migrate to Mexico in the fall [.] Are Monarchs in Michigan in winter [?]
> Monarchs are not in Michigan in winter.
> Orangutans live in a small part of Southeast Asia [.] The Brazilian rain forest is in South America [.] Do orangutans live in the Brazilian rain forest [?]
> Orangutans live in the Brazilian rain forest.
>
> ○ **Review Work**
> Choose one declarative sentence from each group of sentences. Underline the complete subject once. Underline the complete predicate twice.
>
> ✎ **Draft Book**
> Write your own set of interrogative and declarative sentences. Begin each sentence with an uppercase letter and end it with the correct punctuation mark.
>
> **88** CD-4338 Grammar Rules! Grades 3–4   © Carson-Dellosa

RW: Answers will vary. DB: Answers will vary.

Page 89

> Name _____
>
> ### ▶ Wow!   exclamatory sentences
>
> An exclamatory sentence shows strong feelings and ends with an exclamation mark.
> **Rewrite each exclamatory sentence. Put uppercase letters where they belong and exclamation marks at the ends.**
>
> this dessert is delicious
> This dessert is delicious!
> that comet is breathtaking
> That comet is breathtaking!
> we're going to florida
> We're going to Florida!
> ouch, get off my foot
> Ouch, get off my foot!
> you startled me
> You startled me!
> the fireworks are incredible
> The fireworks are incredible!
> i did not crack that plate
> I did not crack that plate!
>
> ○ **Review Work**
> Choose one sentence from above and draw a star next to it. Pretend that sentence is the answer and write a question for it.
>
> ✎ **Draft Book**
> Write five exclamatory sentences. Begin each sentence with an uppercase letter and end it with an exclamation mark.
>
> © Carson-Dellosa   CD-4338 Grammar Rules! Grades 3–4   **89**

RW: Answers will vary. DB: Answers will vary.

Page 90

> Name _____
>
> ### ▶ Amusement Park   declarative, interrogative, and exclamatory sentences
>
> A declarative sentence tells something and ends with a period. An interrogative sentence asks a question and ends with a question mark. An exclamatory sentence shows strong feelings and ends with an exclamation mark.
> **Put the correct punctuation mark at the end of each sentence. Write declarative, interrogative, or exclamatory on the line.**
>
> our class is going to the amusement park [.] _declarative_
> the bus will leave early [.] _declarative_
> did you set your alarm clock [?] _interrogative_
> abby and i stood in line together [.] _declarative_
> yikes, the food here is expensive [!] _exclamatory_
> did you bring lunch [?] _interrogative_
> i'm glad i did [.] _declarative_
> we put our lunches into lockers [.] _declarative_
> let's go to the rides [!] _exclamatory_
> mona, julie, max, and i get in line for a roller coaster [.] _declarative_
> we put on our seat belts and harnesses [.] _declarative_
> i'm scared [!] _exclamatory_
>
> ○ **Review Work**
> Review the sentence for words that should start with uppercase letters. Cross out the lowercase letters and write the uppercase letters above them.
>
> ✎ **Draft Book**
> Write three declarative, three interrogative, and three exclamatory sentences. Begin each sentence with an uppercase letter and end it with the correct punctuation mark.
>
> **90** CD-4338 Grammar Rules! Grades 3–4   © Carson-Dellosa

RW: Add uppercase letters.
DB: Answers will vary.

Page 91

▶ Now Do This — imperative sentences

A sentence that tells you what to do or gives you a command is called an imperative sentence. An imperative sentence usually ends with a period.

Rewrite these imperative sentences. Put an uppercase letter at the beginning of each sentence and a period at the end.

buckle your seat belt
Buckle your seat belt.

obey traffic signals
Obey traffic signals.

put on your helmet before riding your bike
Put on your helmet before riding your bike.

start all sentences with uppercase letters
Start all sentences with uppercase letters.

turn off those lights
Turn off those lights.

always capitalize proper nouns
Always capitalize proper nouns.

finish your work
Finish your work.

put a period at the end of a declarative sentence
Put a period at the end of a declarative sentence.

Review Work
Underline the verbs in the sentences with blue.

Draft Book
Write five imperative sentences. Begin each sentence with an uppercase letter and end it with a period.

© Carson-Dellosa   CD-4338 Grammar Rules! Grades 3–4   **91**

RW: Underline buckle, obey, put, start, turn, capitalize, finish, and put with blue.
DB: Answers will vary.

Page 92

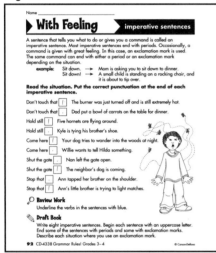

▶ With Feeling — imperative sentences

A sentence that tells you what to do or gives you a command is called an imperative sentence. Most imperative sentences end with periods. Occasionally, a command is given with great feeling. In this case, an exclamation mark is used. The same command can end with either a period or an exclamation mark depending on the situation.

example: Sit down. → Mom is asking you to sit down to dinner.
Sit down! → A small child is standing on a rocking chair, and it is about to tip over.

Read the situation. Put the correct punctuation at the end of each imperative sentence.

Don't touch that [!]   The burner was just turned off and is still extremely hot.
Don't touch that [.]   Dad put a bowl of carrots on the table for dinner.
Hold still [!]   Five hornets are flying around.
Hold still [.]   Kyle is tying his brother's shoe.
Come here [!]   Your dog tries to wander into the woods at night.
Come here [.]   Willie wants to tell Hilda something.
Shut the gate [.]   Nan left the gate open.
Shut the gate [!]   The neighbor's dog is coming.
Stop that [.]   Ann tapped her brother on the shoulder.
Stop that [!]   Ann's little brother is trying to light matches.

Review Work
Underline the verbs in the sentences with blue.

Draft Book
Write eight imperative sentences. Begin each sentence with an uppercase letter. End some of the sentences with periods and some with exclamation marks. Describe each situation where you use an exclamation mark.

92 CD-4338 Grammar Rules! Grades 3–4   © Carson-Dellosa

RW: Underline do touch, was turned, is, do touch, put, hold, are flying, hold, is tying, come, tries, come, wants, shut, left, shut, is coming, stop, tapped, stop, and is trying.
DB: Answers will vary.

Page 93

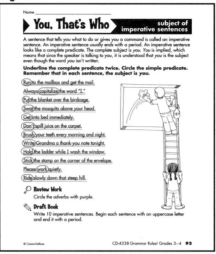

▶ You, That's Who — subject of imperative sentences

A sentence that tells you what to do or gives you a command is an imperative sentence. An imperative sentence usually ends with a period. An imperative sentence looks like a declarative sentence. The complete subject is *you*. You is implied, which means that since the speaker is talking to you, it is understood that *you* is the subject even though the word *you* isn't written.

Underline the complete predicate twice. Circle the simple predicate. Remember that in each sentence, the subject is *you*.

(Run) to the mailbox and get the mail.
Always (capitalize) the word "I."
(Put) the blanket over the birdcage.
(Swat) the mosquito above your head.
(Get) into bed immediately.
(Don't spill) juice on the carpet.
(Brush) your teeth every morning and night.
(Write) Grandma a thank-you note tonight.
(Hold) the ladder while I wash the window.
(Stick) the stamp on the corner of the envelope.
Please (work) quietly.
(Ride) slowly down that steep hill.

Review Work
Circle the adverbs with purple.

Draft Book
Write 10 imperative sentences. Begin each sentence with an uppercase letter and end it with a period.

© Carson-Dellosa   CD-4338 Grammar Rules! Grades 3–4   **93**

RW: Circle always, immediately, morning, night, tonight, quietly, and slowly with purple.
DB: Answers will vary.

Page 94

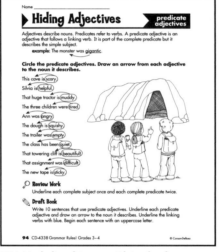

▶ Hiding Adjectives — predicate adjectives

Adjectives describe nouns. Predicates refer to verbs. A predicate adjective is an adjective that follows a linking verb. It is part of the complete predicate but it describes the simple subject.

example: The monster was gigantic.

Circle the predicate adjectives. Draw an arrow from each adjective to the noun it describes.

This cave is (scary).
Silvia is (helpful).
That huge tractor is (muddy).
The three children were (tired).
Ann was (angry).
The dough is (squishy).
The trailer was (empty).
The class has been (quiet).
That towering cliff is (beautiful).
That assignment was (difficult).
The new tape is (sticky).

Review Work
Underline each complete subject once and each complete predicate twice.

Draft Book
Write 10 sentences that use predicate adjectives. Underline each predicate adjective and draw an arrow to the noun it describes. Underline the linking verbs with blue. Begin each sentence with an uppercase letter.

94 CD-4338 Grammar Rules! Grades 3–4   © Carson-Dellosa

RW: Underline this cave, Silvia, that huge tractor, the three children, Ann, the dough, the trailer, the class, that towering cliff, that assignment, and the new tape. Underline is scary, is helpful, is muddy, were tired, was angry, is squishy, was empty, has been quiet, is beautiful, was difficult, and is sticky twice.
DB: Answers will vary.

Page 95

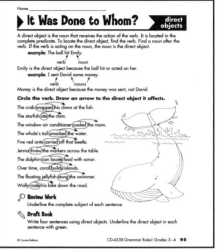

▶ It Was Done to Whom? — direct objects

A direct object is the noun that receives the action of the verb. It is located in the complete predicate. To locate the direct object, find the verb. Find a noun after the verb. If the verb is acting on the noun, the noun is the direct object.

example: The ball hit Emily.
Emily is the direct object because the ball hit or acted on her.

example: I sent David some money.
Money is the direct object because the money was sent, not David.

Circle the verb. Draw an arrow to the direct object it affects.

The crab (snapped) his claws at the fish.
The starfish (ate) the clam.
The window air conditioner (cooled) the room.
The whale's tail (smacked) the water.
Five red ants (carried) off that beetle.
Jenna (threw) the markers across the table.
The dolphin (can locate) food with sonar.
Over time, coral (builds) islands.
The floating jellyfish (stung) the swimmer.
Wally (rode) his bike down the road.

Review Work
Underline the complete subject of each sentence.

Draft Book
Write four sentences using direct objects. Underline the direct object in each sentence with green.

© Carson-Dellosa   CD-4338 Grammar Rules! Grades 3–4   **95**

RW: Underline the crab, the starfish, the window air conditioner, the whale's tail, five red ants, Jenna, the dolphin, coral, the floating jellyfish, and Wally. DB: Answers will vary.

Page 96

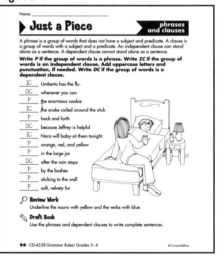

▶ Just a Piece — phrases and clauses

A phrase is a group of words that does not have a subject and predicate. A clause is a group of words with a subject and a predicate. An independent clause can stand alone as a sentence. A dependent clause cannot stand alone as a sentence.

Write P if the group of words is a phrase. Write IC if the group of words is an independent clause. Add uppercase letters and punctuation, if needed. Write DC if the group of words is a dependent clause.

IC   Umberto has the flu.
DC   whenever you can
P   the enormous cookie
IC   the snake coiled around the stick.
P   back and forth
DC   because Jeffrey is helpful
IC   Nora will baby-sit them tonight.
P   orange, red, and yellow
P   in the large jar
DC   after the rain stops
P   by the bushes
P   sticking to the wall
P   soft, velvety fur

Review Work
Underline the nouns with yellow and the verbs with blue.

Draft Book
Use the phrases and dependent clauses to write complete sentences.

96 CD-4338 Grammar Rules! Grades 3–4   © Carson-Dellosa

RW: Underline Umberto, flu, cookie, snake, stick, Jeffrey, Nora, jar, rain, bushes, wall, and fur with yellow. Underline has, can, coiled, is, will baby-sit, and sticking with blue.
DB: Answers will vary.

Page 97

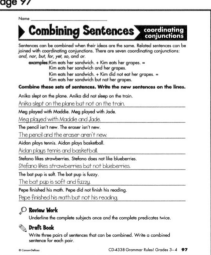

▶ Combining Sentences — coordinating conjunctions

Sentences can be combined when their ideas are the same. Related sentences can be joined with coordinating conjunctions. There are seven coordinating conjunctions: *and, nor, but, for, yet, so,* and *or.*

examples: Kim eats her sandwich. + Kim eats her grapes. =
Kim eats her sandwich and her grapes.
Kim eats her sandwich. + Kim did not eat her grapes. =
Kim eats her sandwich but not her grapes.

Combine these sets of sentences. Write the new sentences on the lines.

Anika slept on the plane. Anika did not sleep on the train.
Anika slept on the plane but not on the train.

Meg played with Maddie. Meg played with Jade.
Meg played with Maddie and Jade.

The pencil isn't new. The eraser isn't new.
The pencil and the eraser aren't new.

Aidan plays tennis. Aidan plays basketball.
Aidan plays tennis and basketball.

Stefano likes strawberries. Stefano does not like blueberries.
Stefano likes strawberries but not blueberries.

The bat pup is soft. The bat pup is fuzzy.
The bat pup is soft and fuzzy.

Pepe finished his math. Pepe did not finish his reading.
Pepe finished his math but not his reading.

Review Work
Underline the complete subjects once and the complete predicates twice.

Draft Book
Write three pairs of sentences that can be combined. Write a combined sentence for each pair.

© Carson-Dellosa   CD-4338 Grammar Rules! Grades 3–4   **97**

Page 97 (cont.)

RW: Underline Anika, Meg, the pencil and the eraser, Aidan, Stefano, the bat pup, and Pepe once. Underline slept on the plane but not on the train, played with Maddie and Jade, aren't new, plays tennis and basketball, likes strawberries but not blueberries, is soft and fuzzy, and finished his math but not his reading twice. DB: Answers will vary.

Page 98

RW: Underline ants and bees, penguins but not polar bears, Alison and Eve, Paul but not Mary, the little gray duck and the baby swan, and starfish and anemones once. Underline live in communities, live in Antarctica, climbed the stairs, read that book, swam in the pond, and live in the ocean twice. DB: Answers will vary.

Page 99

RW: Underline Hal, garden, bird, insects, Renee, ice, snake, grass, chocolate, Nola, picture, Ian, and balloon with yellow. Underline weeded, watered, caught, ate, slipped, fell, slid, slithered, warmed, melted, hangs, straightens, filled, and threw with blue. DB: Answers will vary.

Page 100

RW: Underline Joey, Olivia, Gwen, monkey, thief, carpet, couch, ants, beetles, Mia, candies, peanuts, bedroom, living room, Melea, and Rhonda with yellow. Underline walk, grabbed, climbed, hit, pounded, grabbed, ran, need, scurried, hid, grabs, slams, fell, rolled, are, swim, and dive with blue.
DB: Answers will vary.

Page 101

RW: Underline teddy bear, doll, pillow, Rita, Erlina, slide, lion, tiger, cages, car, van, horsefly, mosquito, door, snail, goldfish, aquarium, hot tub, pool, Roland, Gerald, music, beat, hot dogs, marshmallows, campfire, pajamas, and slippers with yellow. Draw arrows from twisty, their, gray, white, large, buzzing, open, large, orange, black, this, fast, juicy, puffy, white, blue, and fuzzy to the nouns they modify.
DB: Answers will vary.

Page 102

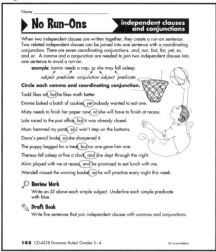

RW: Write an SS above Todd, he, Emmie, nobody, Misty, she, Lola, it, Mom, I, pencil, she, puppy, one, Theresa, she, Alvin, he, Wendell, and he. Underline likes, likes, baked, wanted, needs, will have, raced, was closed, hemmed, will step, broke, sharpened, begged, gave, fell, slept, played, promised, missed, and will practice with blue. DB: Answers will vary.

Page 103

RW: Underline Jade, starfish, sun, shoulders, Zoe, question, Hope, sandwiches, Rob, snow, Jill, snowman, class, rocks, Ali, and fossil with yellow. Underline caught, did keep, was, burned, answered, were, had, gave, was, made, was studying, and brought with blue.
DB: Answers will vary.

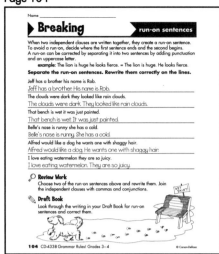

Breaking — run-on sentences

When two independent clauses are written together, they create a run-on sentence. To avoid a run-on, decide where the first sentence ends and the second begins. A run-on can be corrected by separating it into two sentences by adding punctuation and an uppercase letter.

example: The lion is huge he looks fierce. = The lion is huge. He looks fierce.

Separate the run-on sentences. Rewrite them correctly on the lines.

Jeff has a brother his name is Rob.
Jeff has a brother. His name is Rob.
The clouds were dark they looked like rain clouds.
The clouds were dark. They looked like rain clouds.
That bench is wet it was just painted.
That bench is wet. It was just painted.
Belle's nose is runny she has a cold.
Belle's nose is runny. She has a cold.
Alfred would like a dog he wants one with shaggy hair.
Alfred would like a dog. He wants one with shaggy hair.
I love eating watermelon they are so juicy.
I love eating watermelon. They are so juicy.

Review Work
Choose two of the run-on sentences above and rewrite them. Join the independent clauses with commas and conjunctions.

Draft Book
Look through the writing in your Draft Book for run-on sentences and correct them.

104 CD-4338 Grammar Rules! Grades 3–4   © Carson-Dellosa

RW: Answers will vary. DB: Answers will vary.

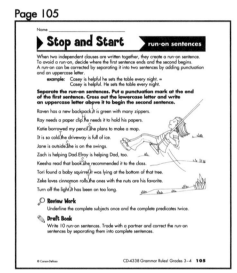

Stop and Start — run-on sentences

When two independent clauses are written together, they create a run-on sentence. To avoid a run-on, decide where the first sentence ends and the second begins. A run-on can be corrected by separating it into two sentences by adding punctuation and an uppercase letter.

example: Casey is helpful he sets the table every night. =
Casey is helpful. He sets the table every night.

Separate the run-on sentences. Put a punctuation mark at the end of the first sentence. Cross out the lowercase letter and write an uppercase letter above it to begin the second sentence.

Raven has a new backpack it is green with many zippers.
Ray needs a paper clip he needs it to hold his papers.
Katie borrowed my pencil she plans to make a map.
It is so cold the driveway is full of ice.
Jane is outside she is on the swings.
Zach is helping Dad Elroy is helping Dad, too.
Keesha read that book she recommended it to the class.
Tori found a baby squirrel it was lying at the bottom of that tree.
Zeke loves cinnamon rolls the ones with the nuts are his favorite.
Turn off the light it has been on too long.

Review Work
Underline the complete subjects once and the complete predicates twice.

Draft Book
Write 10 run-on sentences. Trade with a partner and correct the run-on sentences by separating them into complete sentences.

© Carson-Dellosa   CD-4338 Grammar Rules! Grades 3–4   105

RW: Underline Raven, it, Ray, he, Katie, she, it, the driveway, Jane, she, Zach, Elroy, Keesha, she, Tori, it, Zeke, the ones with nuts, (you), and it once. Underline has a new backpack; is green with many zippers; needs a paper clip; needs it to hold his papers; borrowed my pencil; plans to make a map; is so cold; is full of ice; is outside; is on the swings; is helping Dad; is helping Dad, too; read that book; recommended it to the class; found a baby squirrel; was lying at the bottom of that tree; loves cinnamon rolls; are his favorite; turn off the light; and has been on too long twice.
DB: Answers will vary.

What Do We Have Here? — commas in a series

Commas are used to group three or more common words.
nouns = Abby, Jena, and Zack went skiing.
verbs = Max can race, hurdle, and jump.
adjectives = This muddy, red, cotton shirt should be washed in cold water.
adverbs = The bee flew over, under, and around our desks.

Circle each comma. Write whether it is separating nouns, verbs, adjectives, or adverbs.

Jeff slowly, quietly, and carefully tiptoes past the sleeping baby.   adverbs
Melanie drew a picture of the large, bright, sunny yard.   adjectives
The golf ball bounced, rolled, and dropped into the cup.   verbs
Tanya gulped the glass of fresh, icy, sour lemonade.   adjectives
Bruce saw emeralds, garnets, and rubies in the glass case.   nouns
Leah rolled, folded, and taped the paper around the present.   verbs
I love fresh, warm, crisp chocolate chip cookies.   adjectives
Fred, Benny, Willow, and Bria watched the movie.   nouns
Sign your name slowly, carefully, yet quickly.   adverbs
They played, swam, and ate at the beach.   verbs
Willie was cranky, tired, and hungry.   adjectives
Sam peeled, dipped, and ate the shrimp.   verbs

Review Work
Find the sentence with predicate adjectives. Draw a star next to it.

Draft Book
Write 10 sentences each with a list of three or more nouns. Put commas between the words in the lists.

106 CD-4338 Grammar Rules! Grades 3–4   © Carson-Dellosa

RW: Draw a star next to sentence eleven.
DB: Answers will vary.

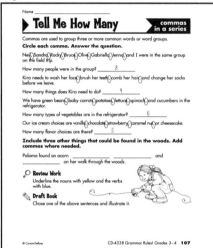

Tell Me How Many — commas in a series

Commas are used to group three or more common words or word groups.
Circle each comma. Answer the question.

Neil, Sandra, Rocky, Bruce, Olive, Gabriella, Jenna, and I were in the same group on the field trip.
How many people were in the group?   8
Kira needs to wash her face, brush her teeth, comb her hair, and change her socks before we leave.
How many things does Kira need to do?   4
We have green beans, baby carrots, potatoes, lettuce, spinach, and cucumbers in the refrigerator.
How many types of vegetables are in the refrigerator?   6
Our ice cream choices are vanilla, chocolate, strawberry, caramel nut, or cheesecake.
How many flavor choices are there?   5

Include three other things that could be found in the woods. Add commas where needed.
Paloma found an acorn, _____, and _____ on her walk through the woods.

Review Work
Underline the nouns with yellow and the verbs with blue.

Draft Book
Chose one of the above sentences and illustrate it.

© Carson-Dellosa   CD-4338 Grammar Rules! Grades 3–4   107

Answers will vary.
RW: Underline Neil, Sandra, Rocky, Bruce, Olive, Gabriella, Jenna, group, field trip, people, group, Kira, face, teeth, hair, socks, things, Kira, green beans, carrots, potatoes, lettuce, spinach, cucumbers, refrigerator, types, vegetables, refrigerator, choices, and choices with yellow. Underline were, were, needs, wash, brush, comb, change, does, have, are, are, and are with blue.
DB: Answers will vary.

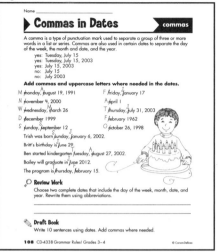

Commas in Dates — commas

A comma is a type of punctuation mark used to separate a group of three or more words in a list or series. Commas are also used in certain dates to separate the day of the week, the month and date, and the year.

yes: Tuesday, July 15
yes: Tuesday, July 15, 2003
yes: July 15, 2003
no: July 15
no: July 2003

Add commas and uppercase letters where needed in the dates.

monday, august 19, 1991   friday, january 17
november 4, 2000   April 1
wednesday, march 26   thursday, july 31, 2003
december 1999   february 1962
sunday, september 12   october 26, 1998
Trish was born sunday, january 6, 2002.
Britt's birthday is june 29.
Ben started kindergarten tuesday, august 27, 2002.
Bailey will graduate in june 2012.
The program is thursday, february 15.

Review Work
Choose two complete dates that include the day of the week, month, date, and year. Rewrite them using abbreviations.

Draft Book
Write 10 sentences using dates. Add commas where needed.

108 CD-4338 Grammar Rules! Grades 3–4   © Carson-Dellosa

RW: Answers will vary. DB: Answers will vary.

Now Read This — quotation marks

Some titles need quotation marks around them.
article titles from magazines and newspapers: I read "Drums Are Beating" in the Wednesday paper.
chapter titles in a book: The chapter "Moon Phases" was interesting.
song and poem titles: We sang "Row, Row, Row Your Boat" in music today.
Book titles, however, do not need quotation marks. Book titles are underlined.

Add quotation marks where they belong. Underline book titles.

The chapter "Summertime" in the book A Year with Me talked about gardening.
I will read "No Bikes Allowed" when you hand me the newspaper.
The headline on this page says "Meteor Shower Tonight."
Iris played "Marching Along" on her flute.
Zane's favorite song is "Tennis Shoe Run."
Did you read Evermore Evening? I'm on the fifth chapter called "Stars Come Out."
You should read this article called "How to Be Nice to Your Little Sister."
Ernie's birds like to sing when "Birdie Bop" plays on the radio.
I think the poem "Bellybutton" is funny.
Kale's favorite book is Up and Down.

Review Work
Underline the simple predicates with blue.

Draft Book
Write eight sentences using titles. Use the skill learned on this page to punctuate titles.

© Carson-Dellosa   CD-4338 Grammar Rules! Grades 3–4   109

RW: Underline talked, read, says, played, is, read, read, like, think, and is with blue.
DB: Answers will vary.

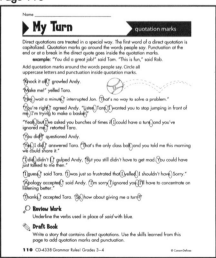

My Turn — quotation marks

Direct quotations are treated in a special way. The first word of a direct quotation is capitalized. Quotation marks go around the words people say. Punctuation at the end or at a break in the direct quote goes inside the quotation marks.

example: "You did a great job!" said Tom. "This is fun," said Rob.

Add quotation marks around the words people say. Circle all uppercase letters and punctuation inside quotation marks.

"Knock it off," growled Andy.
"Make me!" yelled Tara.
"Hey, wait a minute," interrupted Jon. "That's no way to solve a problem."
"You're right," agreed Andy. "Listen, Tara, I wanted to stop jumping in front of me. I'm trying to make a basket."
"Yeah, but I've asked you bunches of times if I could have a turn and you've ignored me," retorted Tara.
"You did?" questioned Andy.
"Yes, I did," answered Tara. "That's the only class ball and you told me this morning we could share it."
"I didn't," gulped Andy. "But you still didn't have to get mad. You could have just talked to me then."
"I guess," said Tara. "I was just so frustrated that I yelled. I shouldn't have. Sorry."
"Apology accepted," said Andy. "I'm sorry I ignored you. I'll have to concentrate on listening better."
"Thanks," accepted Tara. "So, how about giving me a turn?"

Review Work
Underline the verbs used in place of said with blue.

Draft Book
Write a story that contains direct quotations. Use the skills learned from this page to add quotation marks and punctuation.

110 CD-4338 Grammar Rules! Grades 3–4   © Carson-Dellosa

RW: Underline growled, yelled, interrupted, agreed, retorted, questioned, answered, gulped, and accepted with blue.